THE FORERUNNER –
JOHN THE BAPTIST

The Forerunner —
John the Baptist

MARK ALLFREE

THE CHRISTADELPHIAN
404 Shaftmoor Lane
Hall Green
Birmingham B28 8SZ

2008

First published 2008

ISBN 978-0-85189-181-1

Printed and bound by:

THE CROMWELL PRESS
Trowbridge
Wiltshire BA14 0XB

CONTENTS

CHARTS & ILLUSTRATIONS

FOREWORD

THE divinely appointed role fulfilled by John the Baptist was simply expressed by the prophet Isaiah seven hundred years before John's birth:

"Prepare ye the way of the LORD, make straight in the desert a highway for our God."   (Isaiah 40:3)

John therefore came as a voice crying in the wilderness, with a divine message after four hundred years of prophetic silence. Amidst the darkness of a largely faithless generation, he shone as a burning and shining light, revealing what God expected of His people: repentance of their sins and trust in His purpose.

This preparation created the conditions for John's most remarkable declaration, as he looked on Jesus both before and after his baptism:

"Behold the Lamb of God, which taketh away the sin of the world ... Behold the Lamb of God!"

(John 1:29,36)

For though John could call men and women to repent, only Jesus was able to forgive their sins, and as the Lamb of God he provided the basis of that forgiveness when he laid down his life as a willing sacrifice.

With the coming of Jesus, John's work was eclipsed. "He must increase, but I must decrease", John perceptively remarked. This humble submissiveness should not mask the importance of John's work. He blazed a trail for the one greater than he, whose sandals he was not worthy to unloose. By his efforts large numbers of men and women confronted their own sinfulness. Having confessed their sins, they were led to one sent by God who is "faithful and just to forgive us our sins, and to cleanse us from all unrighteousness" (1 John 1:9).

JOHN THE BAPTIST

His work complete, John's captivity under Herod and his execution plotted by an embittered member of the ruling classes bears an uncanny resemblance to the fate of his Lord about a year later. He truly prepared the way, and in the process left an inspiring example for all who learn about him.

By considering the work of John the Baptist we are led step by step to confront the Lord Jesus Christ and the challenge of his call. John prepared the way, and Jesus calls men and women to follow him in that 'way'. Here is the value of this book, whose theme and subject matter is commended to all readers.

MICHAEL ASHTON
BIRMINGHAM, 2008

1

GABRIEL'S APPEARANCE TO ZACHARIAS

"For I say unto you, Among those that are born of women there is not a greater prophet than John the Baptist: but he that is least in the kingdom of God is greater than he." (Luke 7:28)

THIS was the assessment of the Lord Jesus Christ of John the Baptist. There was no greater prophet than he. Yet we tend to neglect the life of this great man. We consider him as being very much overshadowed by the Lord, and by doing so we are guilty of underestimating his importance and his status in God's eyes. This study is an attempt to look afresh at the life of John, and hopefully to enrich our appreciation of the life of this truly great man.

The family of John

The record in Luke chapter 1 tells us:

"There was in the days of Herod, the king of Judaea, a certain priest named Zacharias, of the course of Abia: and his wife was of the daughters of Aaron, and her name was Elisabeth." (verse 5)

Here we are introduced to the parents of John the Baptist. We learn that Zacharias was a priest, of the course of Abia. This has reference to the days of king David, when the priesthood was divided into twenty-four courses. Each course was to take it in turns to officiate in the service of the sanctuary. Only three or four of the ancient Davidic courses had returned from captivity in Babylon, but the original arrangement was preserved, the names of the original courses according to 1 Chronicles 24 were retained, and priests who returned from captivity were allocated to the various courses by lot.*

---

* A. Edersheim, *The Life and Times of Jesus the Messiah*, page 95.

The course of Abia was the eighth course, according to 1 Chronicles 24:10. That Zacharias belonged to the eighth course is significant – the number eight in scripture speaks of a new beginning. For example, there were "eight souls" (1 Peter 3:20) and Noah was "the eighth person" (2 Peter 2:5) who came out of the ark to a renewed earth. Jesus Christ rose from the dead to newness of life on the first day of the week, also the eighth day. Here then was an indication that a new era in the purpose of God was about to begin. Perhaps it is also significant that the ninth course was the course of Jeshua (1 Chronicles 24:11), the Hebrew name for Jesus: the ministry of John the Baptist was to herald that of the Lord Jesus.

Elisabeth

Zacharias' wife was Elisabeth. She too was of the daughters of Aaron. Not only was Zacharias a priest, but also he had married a direct descendant of Aaron. This was not a requirement of the Law of Moses. The law merely stipulated that a priest should not marry a harlot, a profane woman, or a woman put away from her husband (Leviticus 21:7). Even the high priest was only required to marry an Israelite virgin, not necessarily of the tribe of Levi (verse 14)*, but Zacharias had married a priest's daughter.

Whilst Elisabeth was of the daughters of Aaron, she was also related to Mary the mother of the Lord, who was of the tribe of Judah. Brother Thomas suggests that Jesus and John were second cousins:

"Jesus, the grandson of Heli, being born of Joseph's wife, was born hereditary king of the Jews. Heli married the sister of the father of Elizabeth, the wife of Zechariah, and mother of John the Baptizer, who

* It is interesting to observe that those mortal members of the tribe of Levi who will officiate in the sanctuary in the age to come will also not be permitted to marry "a widow, nor her that is put away: but they shall take maidens of the seed of the house of Israel, or a widow that had a priest before" (Ezekiel 44:22).

2

was, therefore, second cousin to Jesus. Elizabeth was of the daughters of Aaron; consequently Mary, daughter of Heli and mother of Jesus, was of the house of David by her father, and of the house of Aaron by her mother: so that in her son Jesus was not only vested, by his birth and the marriage of his mother, all kingly rights, but all rego-pontifical as well. In Jesus, therefore, is united the combined kingly and high-priestly offices of the nation of Israel: so that when the government shall be upon his shoulders he will sit as a priest upon his throne, after the order of Melchizedek, without predecessor or successor in the united office of king and priest."*

It is interesting to note that Aaron himself married a wife called Elisheba, which is essentially the same name as Elisabeth:

"And Aaron took him Elisheba, daughter of Amminadab, sister of Naashon, to wife; and she bare him Nadab, and Abihu, Eleazar, and Ithamar."

(Exodus 6:23)

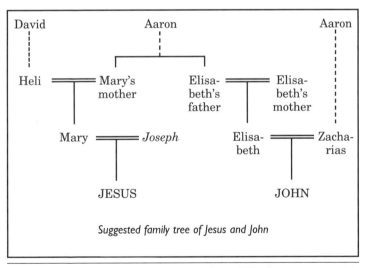

Suggested family tree of Jesus and John

---

* Robert Roberts, *Dr. Thomas, his Life and Work*, pages 119,120, Fourth Edition.

3

This Elisheba, or Elisabeth, was not a Levite, but was of the tribe of Judah. Thus, as far as the Law of Moses was concerned, the credentials of Zacharias were impeccable – more so in fact than Aaron's himself, because his wife was from Judah. Not only so, but the record tells us that "they were both righteous before God, walking in all the commandments and ordinances of the Lord blameless" (Luke 1:6). So far as man could tell, Zacharias' and Elisabeth's observance of the Law of Moses was without fault. This is not of course to say that they were without sin. The Apostle Paul could say that "touching the righteousness which is in the law" he too was "blameless" (Philippians 3:6). Yet he also described himself as "chief" of sinners because of his persecution of the ecclesia (1 Timothy 1:15).

Whilst it might have been possible to observe the rituals of the law blamelessly, it was nevertheless true that "by the deeds of the law there shall no flesh be justified in his sight: for by the law is the knowledge of sin" (Romans 3:20). In contrast, the Lord Jesus Christ was not blameless touching the law, for through no fault of his own he fell foul of Deuteronomy 21:23: "He that is hanged is accursed of God". Nevertheless the scriptures tell us that he "did no sin, neither was guile found in his mouth" (1 Peter 2:22).

Not only were their credentials impeccable, but they also kept the law blamelessly. Yet, in spite of their faithfulness to the law, they were denied the blessing of children, and they were old. The law was impotent to give them what they really wanted more than anything:

"And they had no child, because that Elisabeth was barren, and they both were now well stricken in years." (Luke 1:7)

Elisabeth barren

There is a very obvious connection here with the lives of Abraham and Sarah:

4

"Now Abraham and Sarah were old and well stricken in age; and it ceased to be with Sarah after the manner of women." (Genesis 18:11)

We can see that the circumstances in these two families are remarkably similar. In fact the similarity extends further, because when Abraham was told that he would have a son, Sarah disbelieved:

"Therefore Sarah laughed within herself, saying, After I am waxed old shall I have pleasure, my lord being old also?" (Genesis 18:12)

In due course Zacharias also expressed his disbelief when Gabriel told him he would have a son.

Nevertheless in the fullness of time, Abraham and Sarah had a son Isaac. The scriptures go out of their way to tell us that Isaac was a child of promise. Paul in Galatians for example contrasts Isaac with Ishmael, and says that "he who was of the bondwoman was born after the flesh; but he of the freewoman was *by promise*" (Galatians 4:23). Similarly, Paul in Romans reminds us that "this is the word *of promise*, At this time will I come, and Sarah shall have a son" (Romans 9:9).

What does this teach us about John? Surely that he too would be a child of promise. In fact he would be the means whereby the promises made with Abraham, which incorporate the hope of salvation for mankind, would come to fruition. Zacharias and Elisabeth had impeccable credentials according to the law. They kept the law blamelessly, but they were going to have a son by promise. This is the point that Luke is making – that salvation would come, not through observance of the law, but through the fulfilment of the promises.

This is the overall theme that runs through this first chapter of Luke's Gospel. Jesus said that "the law and the prophets were until John: since that time the kingdom of God is preached" (Luke 16:16). John's ministry was going to usher in a great change in the purpose of God; the epoch of the law was coming to an end.

5

Offering incense in the temple

Zacharias' duty was to burn incense in the temple in Jerusalem:

> "And it came to pass, that while he executed the priest's office before God in the order of his course, according to the custom of the priest's office, his lot was to burn incense when he went into the temple of the Lord." (Luke 1:8,9)

By this time, the priesthood had become so large that there were not enough duties to go round. It has been estimated that there were probably about 20,000 priests at this time,* and that on any one day there would be fifty priests officiating in the temple. The custom of casting lots to determine which priest would perform each function had therefore been adopted. According to Dr. Edersheim, there were four lots cast to determine the ministry for each day.** The first was cast before the break of day to designate those priests who were to cleanse the altar of burnt offering from the ministrations of the previous day, and to prepare its fires. The second lot determined those priests who would prepare the sacrifice, and cleanse the candlestick and the altar of incense. The priest selected by the third lot had the duty of offering the incense. The fourth lot determined those priests who would lay on the altar the sacrifice, the meal offering and the drink offering. The offering of incense was regarded as a great privilege – in fact a priest could not offer incense more than once in his entire lifetime (Mishnah, *Tamid* 5:2). Many priests would not have enjoyed the privilege of offering incense at all. We can thus appreciate that here was the most important moment in the life of Zacharias thus far.

The psalmist tells us very plainly that the offering of incense is symbolic of the offering up of prayer: "Let my prayer be set forth before thee as incense; and the lifting

---

* A. Edersheim, *The Life and Times of Jesus the Messiah*, page 94.
** A. Edersheim, *The Temple, its ministry and services as they were at the time of Jesus Christ*, page 158 ff.

up of my hands as the evening sacrifice" (Psalm 141:2). This emerges in the record in Luke 1 because verse 10 tells us that "the whole multitude of the people were praying without at the time of incense". Clearly Zacharias also prayed whilst offering his incense, because Gabriel said to him in verse 13, "Fear not, Zacharias: for thy prayer is heard".

What did Zacharias pray about?

Under the Law of Moses, very exacting requirements were laid down concerning the manufacture of incense (Exodus 30:34-38). The offering of strange incense was forbidden and punished by death (Leviticus 10:1). The simple lesson from this is that prayer before God must be very carefully prepared. We can imagine that as Zacharias prepared to offer the incense he would also have made meticulous preparations regarding the prayer he would offer whilst in the temple of the Lord.

What do we suppose he prayed about? Clearly he prayed for a son, because Gabriel said: "Thy prayer is heard; and thy wife Elisabeth shall bear thee a son, and thou shalt call his name John". But surely he would also have prayed for the coming of the Messiah. There was an air of expectancy in the nation of Israel at this time. They were expecting the Messiah to come at any time, because they knew that they were living at the end of the period of Daniel's Seventy Weeks prophecy, recorded for us in Daniel 9.

The Seventy Weeks prophecy

The prophecy of the Seventy Weeks was given to Daniel by the angel Gabriel:

"Know therefore and understand, that from the going forth of the commandment to restore and to build Jerusalem unto the Messiah the Prince shall be seven weeks, and threescore and two weeks: the street shall be built again, and the wall, even in troublous times." (Daniel 9:25)

7

The decree issued by Artaxerxes in Ezra 7:13, permitting the Jews to return with Ezra to Jerusalem, is considered to have been issued in 457 BC. Daniel was told that Messiah the Prince would come after "seven weeks, and threescore and two weeks" – that is, a total of sixty-nine weeks, or 483 days. If we accept the principle of one prophetic day representing one year of real time,* then this takes us to AD 26, the year of the manifestation of the Lord Jesus Christ.** Every God-fearing Jew in Israel in the days of Zacharias would have known this. So in those days there would have been a buzz of anticipation as they waited for the Messiah to come.

We know that the angel Gabriel appeared to Zacharias in the temple. It is not a coincidence that the Seventy Weeks prophecy was given to Daniel by Gabriel, as he was praying, at the time of the offering of incense:

> "And whiles I was speaking, and praying, and confessing my sin and the sin of my people Israel, and presenting my supplication before the LORD my God for the holy mountain of my God; yea, whiles I was speaking in prayer, even the man Gabriel, whom I had

---

* This principle is based on Numbers 14:34 and Ezekiel 4:6.

** The chronology of Daniel's Seventy Week prophecy is fraught with difficulty, and there can be little room for dogmatism. There were four decrees issued by Persian kings, in favour of the return of the Jews and the rebuilding of Jerusalem:

1) The 1st year of Cyrus (Ezra 1:1)	538 BC
2) The 2nd year of Darius (Ezra 6:1)	520 BC
3) The 7th year of Artaxerxes (Ezra 7:1,13)	457 BC
4) The 20th year of Artaxerxes (Nehemiah 2:1)	444 BC

Anstey (*Chronology of the Old Testament*, pages 20-24,276-282) advocates the first year of Cyrus, but admits that a discrepancy of some eighty-two years has to be accounted for. Brother Thomas (*Exposition of Daniel*, page 36) considers the decree to be that of the twentieth year of Artaxerxes, although it has to be said that there is no specific mention of a decree in Nehemiah 2. Also, Brother Thomas assumes the twentieth year of Artaxerxes to be 456 BC. Further confusion arises when seeking to identify the Artaxerxes of Nehemiah 2. It is usually considered to be Longimanus, who ruled Persia between 456 and 423 BC. There are

seen in the vision at the beginning, being caused to fly swiftly, touched me about the time of the evening oblation." (Daniel 9:20,21)

What was to be accomplished by the end of the seventy weeks time period? Daniel was told by Gabriel:

"Seventy weeks are determined upon thy people and upon thy holy city, to finish the transgression, and to make an end of sins, and to make reconciliation for iniquity, and to bring in everlasting righteousness, and to seal up the vision and prophecy, and to anoint the most Holy." (Daniel 9:24)

1. "To finish transgression ... sins ... iniquity"

Note that the angel specifically mentions iniquity, transgression and sin. This has echoes in the great day of atonement when the iniquities, transgressions and sins of the nation of Israel were confessed and forgiven (Leviticus 16:21). The day of atonement foreshadowed the sacrificial work of the Lord Jesus Christ, "by whom we have now received the atonement" (Romans 5:11).

2. "To bring in everlasting righteousness"

The death and resurrection of Jesus was a powerful testimony to the righteousness of God (Romans 3:25,26).

---

a number of difficulties with this, however. For example, Ezra would have been over 120 when he returned from Babylon, and over 140 when he walked in procession at the dedication of the wall. It has been suggested that the particular Artaxerxes was Darius Hystaspes, who ruled for thirty-six years from 521 BC. The twentieth year of his reign would thus become 501 BC. But if this is taken as the year of the issuing of the commandment "to restore and to build Jerusalem", then the time to "Messiah the prince" is over forty years too long. Proponents of this view thus have to allow for a correction in the chronological record. It would seem that the simplest approach would be to accept the seventh year of Artaxerxes as the commandment to which the angel Gabriel referred. Ezra 9:9 lends weight to this conclusion: "For we were bondmen; yet our God hath not forsaken us in our bondage, but hath extended mercy unto us in the sight of the kings of Persia, to give us a reviving, to set up the house of our God, and to repair the desolations thereof, and to give us a wall in Judah and in Jerusalem."

9

Righteousness is imputed to those who associate with
the sacrificial work of Jesus by belief and baptism
(Romans 4:5).

3. "To seal up the vision and prophecy"

The RSV renders this, "To seal both vision and prophet".
The reference is to the Lord Jesus Christ, the prophet
like unto Moses (Deuteronomy 18:15), who received the
seal of divine approval (John 6:27).

4. "To anoint the most Holy"

Rotherham translates this, "And anoint the holy of
holies". The reference is again to Jesus who said to the
Jews concerning himself, "Destroy this temple, and in
three days I will raise it up" (John 2:19). Gabriel
described the Lord as "that holy thing" (Luke 1:35). He
was anointed at the beginning of his ministry by the
Holy Spirit (Luke 3:22; Acts 10:38). He was anointed
king when, after the completion of his work of atonement, he was received up into heaven (Psalm 45:7).

Although Daniel was in captivity in Babylon, he was
still living under the jurisdiction of the Law of Moses.
The law was still in force. But none of these things
mentioned by Gabriel could be accomplished by the Law
of Moses. The law could not finish transgressions, or
make an end of sins. The law could not bring in
everlasting righteousness, and Zacharias the priest
knew that. This priest with perfect qualifications knew
that salvation would not be achieved by the law.
Everlasting righteousness, and reconciliation for iniquity
would only be secured by the coming of Messiah the
prince. John the Baptist was to prepare the way for that
great one.

2

THE MINISTRY OF JOHN FORETOLD

"The effectual fervent prayer of a righteous man availeth much." (James 5:16)

THIS was certainly the experience of Zacharias, for whilst he was in the very process of offering his incense and making his prayer to God, the angel Gabriel appeared to him, standing on the right side of the altar of incense.

We can imagine how Zacharias would have felt when Gabriel appeared to him in the privacy of the temple. There had been no direct communication from God since the time of Malachi, about 400 years before, but then suddenly the angel of the Lord appeared to Zacharias. No wonder it says that "he was troubled". But Gabriel had come with a message of hope and encouragement:

"The angel said unto him, Fear not, Zacharias: for thy prayer is heard; and thy wife Elisabeth shall bear thee a son, and thou shalt call his name John."
(Luke 1:13)

It is a testimony to the faithfulness of this couple that they had continued praying for a son, despite their advancing years. Now their faith was to be rewarded by the blessing of a son. He was to be called John – a name ordained of God. Clearly therefore there must be a significance behind this name. John means, "Yah is merciful". It is in fact a reference to the covenants of promise, as we can see from Deuteronomy 7:

"Know therefore that the LORD thy God, he is God, the faithful God, which keepeth covenant and mercy with them that love him and keep his commandments to a thousand generations." (Deuteronomy 7:9)

In the Old Testament, the Abrahamic and Davidic covenants are frequently spoken of as the "mercy" of God. The very name of John indicated that God, who keeps covenant and mercy, was about to perform the truth to Jacob, and the mercy* to Abraham, which He had sworn to the fathers from the days of old (Micah 7:20).

Gabriel's predictions concerning John

In Luke 1:14-17 the angel Gabriel made a number of predictions concerning John:

1. REJOICING AT HIS BIRTH

"And thou shalt have joy and gladness; and many shall rejoice at his birth" (verse 14). So it came to pass, for we read that Elisabeth's "neighbours and her cousins heard how the Lord had shewed great mercy upon her; and they rejoiced with her" (verse 58). Not only was the birth of John to Zacharias and Elisabeth in their old age a joyful event in itself, but also John was to be the forerunner of the Messiah, for whom all the faithful in Israel were eagerly waiting. That the Messiah was soon to come was indeed a great cause for joy and rejoicing.

2. GREAT IN THE SIGHT OF GOD

"For he shall be great in the sight of the Lord ..." (verse 15). It is only written of one other man in the scripture that "he shall be great". That is, of course, the Lord Jesus Christ himself (verse 32). Here is a measure of the greatness of this man John. In the eyes of men the behaviour of John would have seemed foolish in the extreme – living in the desert, wearing camel skins, eating locusts and eschewing all the luxuries of life – but John's greatness was before God, and this is what matters. So great was he before God that Jesus said, "Among them that are born of women there hath not risen a greater than John the Baptist" (Matthew 11:11).

3. NAZARITE

"And shall drink neither wine nor strong drink ..." (Luke 1:15). Under the law, the priests were forbidden to drink

---

* Hebrew, *chesed*. Consider the following: Genesis 24:27; 32:10; Deuteronomy 7:12; 2 Samuel 7:15; 22:51; 1 Kings 8:23; 1 Chronicles 17:13; Nehemiah 1:5; 9:32; Psalm 18:50; 89:1,2,14,24,28; Isaiah 55:3; Daniel 9:4.

wine or strong drink when they went into the tabernacle of the congregation, on pain of death:

"And the LORD spake unto Aaron, saying, Do not drink wine nor strong drink, thou, nor thy sons with thee, when ye go into the tabernacle of the congregation, lest ye die: it shall be a statute for ever throughout your generations."   (Leviticus 10:8,9)

The appearance of this prohibition in the record immediately after the incident of Nadab and Abihu, who died because they "offered strange fire before the LORD" (verses 1-7), suggests that they had been under the influence of strong drink when performing their duties in the tabernacle.* Because of what happened to Nadab and Abihu, this prohibition enjoined upon the priesthood was well known, and was rigidly adhered to. For Gabriel to specify to Zacharias that John, a priest, would drink neither wine nor strong drink, implies that this was something over and above the normal regulation governing the priesthood.

It is likely that this is a reference to the vow of the Nazarite, which is found in Numbers 6. The Nazarite vow was a provision whereby men or women who were not priests were able to dedicate themselves to God in a similar way to the priests. For the period of their Nazariteship they were to:

• Abstain from wine and strong drink (verse 3);
• Refrain from cutting hair (verse 5);
• Abstain from contact with the dead (verse 6).

By so doing they were imitating the conduct of the priesthood. They were separating themselves to Yahweh in a similar way to the priests, and living a life of dedication to God.**

---

* See J. J. Blunt, *Undesigned Scriptural Coincidences*, pages 64-66.
** For a detailed exposition of the Nazarite vow see J. Martin, *The Schoolmaster, an Exposition of the Book of Leviticus*, pages 339-349. Also see W. F. Barling, *Law and Grace*, pages 121-124.

The Nazarite	The priesthood
"He shall separate himself from wine and strong drink" (Numbers 6:3).	"Do not drink wine nor strong drink, thou, nor thy sons with thee" (Leviticus 10:9).
"There shall no razor come upon his head ... because the consecration of his God is upon his head" (Numbers 6:5-7).	"They shall not make baldness upon their head" (Leviticus 21:5). "For the crown (Heb. *nezer*) of the anointing oil of his God is upon him" (verse 12).
"He shall come at no dead body" (Numbers 6:6).	"There shall none be defiled for the dead among his people" (Leviticus 21:1). "Neither shall he go in to any dead body" (verse 11).

John the Baptist was already a priest, but in addition he appears to have taken a Nazarite vow which presumably lasted all his life. In effect he was saying that his life and service was going to be more exemplary than the Levitical priesthood. Furthermore, he was also emphasising that the Levitical priesthood was of itself incapable of securing salvation. Although he was a priest by right, John never served as a priest, and his very appearance was the antithesis of what a man would expect of a priest. He never wore the vestments of the priesthood; instead he chose to dress in desert clothes and eat desert food. The essence of his ministry was to teach that salvation and redemption would not come through the Levitical priesthood, but through the one for whom he was preparing the way.

4. FILLED WITH THE HOLY SPIRIT

"And he shall be filled with the Holy Spirit, even from his mother's womb" (Luke 1:15). As evidence of this, we are told in verse 44 that the babe leaped in his mother's womb for joy when Elisabeth heard the salutation of Mary. In the same way that Jeremiah the prophet had been sanctified before he was born (Jeremiah 1:5), and subsequently the Apostle Paul was separated from his mother's womb (Galatians 1:15), so too John the Baptist was divinely appointed from birth for the great task of preparing the way for the Messiah.

Although he was filled with the Holy Spirit from his mother's womb, we are told in John 10:41 that "John did no miracle". How then was the activity of the Holy Spirit apparent in the life of John? It can only have been through his preaching. With the exception of Jesus himself, John was the greatest preacher of all time – hence his description in the scriptures as "the voice" (Isaiah 40:3; John 1:23).

5. SPIRIT AND POWER OF ELIAS

"And many of the children of Israel shall he turn to the Lord their God. And he shall go before him in the spirit and power of Elias, to turn the hearts of the fathers to the children, and the disobedient to the wisdom of the just; to make ready a people prepared for the Lord." (Luke 1:16,17)

This is a quotation from Malachi chapter 4, where Malachi tells us about the future ministry of Elijah. This is what Elijah also will do:

"Behold, I will send you Elijah the prophet before the coming of the great and dreadful day of the LORD: and he shall turn the heart of the fathers to the children, and the heart of the children to their fathers, lest I come and smite the earth with a curse." (Malachi 4:5,6)

In effect, John was giving to Israel a foretaste of the future ministry of Elijah. This was emphasised by his appearance. Matthew tells us that "John had his raiment of camel's hair, and a leathern girdle about his loins" (Matthew 3:4). Similarly concerning Elijah we are told that he "was a man with a garment of hair (RV margin), and girt with a girdle of leather about his loins" (2 Kings 1:8). When people met John, it was almost as if Elijah was in their midst. This is why Jesus said concerning

15

John, "And if ye will receive it, this is Elias, which was for to come" (Matthew 11:14).

6. HEARTS OF FATHERS TO CHILDREN

The effect of John's ministry would be to "turn the hearts of the fathers to the children, and the disobedient to the wisdom of the just" (Luke 1:17). Gabriel is not just saying that John's preaching would promote harmony between fathers and sons. When we read in scripture of the fathers, we should think primarily of Abraham, Isaac and Jacob.* They are pre-eminently the fathers of the Jewish people. Gabriel is thus saying that by his preaching, John would encourage people to walk in faith, like Abraham, Isaac and Jacob, who were justified by faith – so much so that if the fathers had been in their midst, they would have recognised them as their children.

This will happen one day. We know that Abraham, Isaac and Jacob will stand in the kingdom of God. In that day they will recognise those who share their faith. Isaiah speaks about this in Isaiah 29:

"Therefore thus saith the LORD, who redeemed Abraham, concerning the house of Jacob, Jacob shall not now be ashamed, neither shall his face now wax pale. But when he seeth his children, the work of mine hands, in the midst of him, they shall sanctify my name, and sanctify the Holy One of Jacob, and shall fear the God of Israel." (verses 22,23)

John the Baptist was to begin this process of persuading Jacob's children to walk in faith, like the fathers of old. The disobedient in the nation would be brought to repentance, so much so that they would walk in "the wisdom of the just". Again, this is not just a general statement from the mouth of Gabriel, but a reference to Abraham, who was justified by faith; he believed God, and his belief was counted to him for righteousness (Genesis 15:6; Romans 4:9,22). A

* See, for example, Luke 1:55,72; Acts 3:25; 7:32; 13:32; 26:6; Romans 9:5; 15:8; Hebrews 8:9; 2 Peter 3:4.

comparison between Malachi 4:6 and Luke 1:17 confirms that the fathers correspond to "the just" and the children to "the disobedient". This supports the conclusion that by "the fathers" we are intended to call to mind the great patriarchs of old.

Malachi 4:6	Luke 1:17
"And he shall turn the heart of the fathers to the children ..."	"To turn the hearts of the fathers to the children ..."
"... and the heart of the children ..."	"... and the disobedient ..."
"to their fathers"	"... to the wisdom of the just"

Once again we can see that the thrust of John's teaching would be that salvation was not to be achieved through the works of the law, but rather justification would be by faith, as it was for Abraham. This message is emphasised by what happened next in Luke 1.

"Thou shalt be dumb"

Zacharias was so overawed by the occasion that his faith momentarily let him down:

> "And Zacharias said unto the angel, Whereby shall I know this? for I am an old man, and my wife well stricken in years. And the angel answering said unto him, I am Gabriel, that stand in the presence of God; and am sent to speak unto thee, and to shew thee these glad tidings. And, behold, thou shalt be dumb, and not able to speak, until the day that these things shall be performed, because thou believest not my words." (Luke 1:18-20)

The irony of this is that Zacharias had just been told he was to have a son. That son would be *a voice crying*. But Zacharias found himself unable to tell anyone the good news because his voice was taken away! Upon leaving the temple, it was customary for the priest to recite the blessing of Numbers 6:24-26 over the congregation, and to this the people would respond with the words, "Blessed be the Lord God, the God of Israel, from everlasting to everlasting",* but all that Zacharias could do was to gesticulate with his hands, to try to make the people understand what had happened. A tremendous contrast is being drawn between Zacharias and John. Zacharias the priest, with impeccable credentials and pedigree, represents the Law of Moses. He was made mute – indicating that the law was soon to pass away; it had served its purpose and would soon be silenced. John the Baptist, the "voice", was about to burst on the scene as a burning and shining light. He would come to prepare the way for the Messiah, who would make an end of sins and bring in everlasting righteousness – not through the law, but through faith in the covenants of promise. This theme is expanded in a wonderful way by Zacharias himself in the psalm that he speaks after the birth of John.

Meanwhile, the days of his ministration completed, Zacharias departed to his home. In due course, in fulfilment of the words of Gabriel, Elisabeth his wife conceived, and hid herself away for five months, perhaps to meditate and to give thanks unto God. Echoing the words of Rachel (Genesis 30:23) after the birth of Joseph, she said, "Thus hath the Lord dealt with me in the days wherein he looked on me, to take away my reproach among men" (Luke 1:25). After this length of time it would have been evident to all that Elisabeth, well known by her acquaintances as the one "who was called barren" (Luke 1:36), was no longer so, for God had made "the barren woman to keep house, and to be a joyful mother of children" (Psalm 113:9).

---

* A. Edersheim, *The Temple, its ministry and services as they were at the time of Jesus Christ*, page 170.

3

THE PSALM OF ZACHARIAS

W
E have seen in the early verses of Luke 1 that the circumstances surrounding the conception of John in his mother's womb indicated that the purpose of God was going to change from law to grace. The birth of John, whose very name means the mercy, or the grace, of Yahweh, signified the fact that the Law of Moses was about to pass away and the covenants of promise would begin to be fulfilled. The law and the prophets were until John.

The birth of John

We move forward now to the actual birth of John, in verses 57-80, where the same theme is presented to us:

"Now Elisabeth's time was fulfilled that she should be delivered; and she brought forth a son. And her neighbours and her kinsfolk heard that the Lord had magnified his mercy towards her; and they rejoiced with her." (Luke 1:57,58, RV)

The key word here again is "mercy". Luke is not simply indicating that God had been kind to Elisabeth. The language used is that of the covenant. Elisabeth was thanking God with her friends that He had seen fit to involve her and her family in the fulfilment of the "truth to Jacob, and the mercy to Abraham", which God had sworn to the fathers from the days of old (Micah 7:20).

Circumcision

The day came for John to be circumcised. This was the eighth day according to Genesis 17:12:

"And he that is eight days old shall be circumcised among you, every man child in your generations, he that is born in the house, or bought with money of any stranger, which is not of thy seed."

19

JOHN THE BAPTIST

This was a ritual that was deep with meaning, the origin of which was traced right back to Abraham himself when it was divinely ordained as a token of the covenant that God had made with him, "a seal of the righteousness of the faith which he had yet being uncircumcised" (Romans 4:11). Because of its Abrahamic origins, and its association with the covenant, the ritual of circumcision was considered to be of such importance to the Jews that if the eighth day fell on a sabbath the ritual of circumcision took precedence over observance of the sabbath. Hence the Lord Jesus Christ's censure of the Jews in his days:

> "Moses therefore gave you circumcision (not because it is of Moses, but of the fathers); and ye on the sabbath day circumcise a man. If a man on the sabbath day receive circumcision, that the law of Moses should not be broken; are ye angry at me, because I have made a man every whit whole on the sabbath day? Judge not according to the appearance, but judge righteous judgment." (John 7:22-24)

Edersheim suggests that when a child was circumcised a prayer was offered beforehand, and the ceremony concluded with a feast and a cup of wine, reflecting the great feast that Abraham held for Isaac when he was weaned (Genesis 21:8). The child would have received his name in a prayer very similar to that used even today by the Jews:

> "Our God, and the God of our fathers, raise up this child to his father and mother, and let his name be called in Israel John, the son of Zacharias. Let his father rejoice in the issue of his loins, and his mother in the fruit of her womb, as it is written in Proverbs 23:25, and as it is said in Ezekiel 16:6, and again in Psalm 105:5, and Genesis 21:4."*

It was common practice in Israel for a son to be named after his father, in much the same way that we tend to

---

* A. Edersheim, *The Life and Times of Jesus the Messiah*, page 111.

20

name our children after ourselves. We can imagine the surprise of those present when Elisabeth insisted that her son was to be called John, which was not a family name (Luke 1:60). They appealed to Zacharias to settle the matter. Verse 62 suggests that Zacharias was deaf as well as dumb, because "they made signs" to him – but he confirmed that his son was to be called John: "And he asked for a writing table, and wrote, saying, His name is John. And they marvelled all" (Luke 1:63).

What a dramatic moment it would have been as Zacharias, who had been deaf and dumb for nine months, opened his mouth and began to speak and to praise God! The theme of the fulfilment of the covenants comes to a head now in this beautiful psalm that Zacharias uttered by means of the Holy Spirit.

Structure

This theme is emphasised by the very structure of the psalm. It contains a sequence of ideas that build up to a climax in verse 72, and those ideas are then restated in reverse order:

- Verse 68 speaks about God visiting His people. The subject of visitation is repeated in verse 78.
- Verse 69 describes how God had raised up a horn of salvation. Verse 77 speaks about giving knowledge of salvation unto His people.
- Verse 70 refers to the holy prophets. Verse 75 says that John himself would be one of those holy prophets.
- Verse 71 speaks of salvation "from our enemies" – a theme repeated in verse 74.
- Verse 72 speaks about the covenants of promise, as does verse 73.

We can thus see that the central climax of this psalm has reference to the covenants of promise. Everything is focusing upon them. Here we have the stamp of divine inspiration, a confirmation that Zacharias was truly "filled with the Holy Spirit" as he prophesied (verse 67).

The structure of the Psalm of Zacharias	
a) Visited and redeemed his people	(verse 68)
b) Horn of salvation	(verse 69)
c) Holy prophets	(verse 70)
d) Salvation from our enemies	(verse 71)
e) *His holy covenant*	(verse 72)
e) *The oath which He sware*	(verse 73)
d) Delivered from our enemies	(verse 74)
c) Prophet of the Highest	(verse 76)
b) Knowledge of salvation to his people	(verse 77)
a) Dayspring from on high hath visited us	(verse 78)

Zacharias, Elisabeth, John

We must remember the underlying reason why this song was given. It was to commemorate the birth of John, who was to prepare the way for the Lord. As it says in verse 76, he was to be "the prophet of the Highest". So the psalm had a very personal relevance to John and his family. In a most remarkable way this emerges in the very climax of the psalm, as the following verses show: "To perform the mercy promised to our fathers, and to remember his holy covenant; the oath which he sware to our father Abraham" (verses 72,73). Hidden in these two verses we have the three names of John, Zacharias and Elisabeth:

- John means "Yahweh is merciful".
- Zacharias means "Yahweh hath remembered".
- Elisabeth means "the oath of God".

At the same time, Zacharias' words were based upon Psalm 105:8-10:

"He hath remembered his covenant for ever, the word which he commanded to a thousand generations. Which covenant he made with Abraham, and his oath unto Isaac; and confirmed the same unto Jacob for a law, and to Israel for an everlasting covenant."

The Spirit was thus signifying in a remarkable way that it had been ordained of old that this small family of believers was to be intimately involved in the fulfilment of the covenants of promise, because John the Baptist was subsequently to prepare the way for none other than the seed of Abraham, the Lord Jesus Christ.

Redemption

Although the covenants lie at the heart of Zacharias' psalm, when we look carefully we can see that the whole psalm revolves around the promises made to the fathers. For example, verses 68 and 69 speak of redemption and salvation, and this theme is echoed in verse 77 where the subject is that of salvation and the remission of sins. This of course is the language of the atonement. Redemption and forgiveness was achieved when the Lord Jesus Christ died on the cross a sinless man, and was raised again for our justification. This is the very essence of the covenant God made with Abraham:

> "By myself have I sworn, saith the LORD, for because thou hast done this thing, and hast not withheld thy son, thine only son: that in blessing I will bless thee, and in multiplying I will multiply thy seed as the stars of the heaven, and as the sand which is upon the sea shore; and thy seed shall possess the gate of his enemies; and in thy seed *shall all the nations of the earth be blessed*; because thou hast obeyed my voice."
>
> (Genesis 22:16-18)

Peter in Acts 3 referred to this blessing available to all nations through Abraham's seed, and explained very clearly that the blessing spoken of was actually that of forgiveness:

> "Ye are the children of the prophets, and of the covenant which God made with our fathers, saying unto Abraham, And in thy seed shall all the kindreds of the earth be blessed. Unto you first God, having raised up his Son Jesus, sent him to bless you, *in turning away every one of you from his iniquities*."
>
> (Acts 3:25,26)

Here, in the very language of the oath God sware to Abraham, we have the doctrine of the atonement.

Enemies

God also said to Abraham in Genesis 22 that "thy seed shall possess the gate of his enemies" (verse 17). Zacharias takes up this part of the Abrahamic covenant when he says:

"That we should be saved from our enemies, and from the hand of all that hate us ... that he would grant unto us, that we being delivered out of the hand of our enemies might serve him without fear."

(Luke 1:71,74)

When Jesus comes again, he will have to subdue his enemies. Psalm 110 tells us that he will rule in the midst of them. Psalm 72:9 goes a step further and says that his enemies will lick the dust. But *the* enemy here is that of sin and death. Psalm 8 comes to mind: "Out of the mouth of babes and sucklings hast thou ordained strength because of thine enemies, that thou mightest still the enemy and the avenger" (verse 2).

Similarly, we read in 1 Corinthians 15 that Jesus must reign "till he hath put all enemies under his feet. The last enemy that shall be destroyed is death" (verses 25,26). It is to that great day that the psalmist looks forward when he says, "I will call upon the LORD, who is worthy to be praised: so shall I be saved from mine enemies" (Psalm 18:3).

Horn of salvation

Luke 1:68 states that God had visited and redeemed His people, and had raised up a horn of salvation in the house of His servant David. So now the Davidic covenant is introduced, and in this connection there are some interesting parallels with Psalm 132.

This psalm tells us how God not only sware to Abraham, but also to David: "The LORD hath sworn in truth unto David; he will not turn from it; of the fruit of thy body will I set upon thy throne" (verse 11). This is a reference to the covenant of 2 Samuel 7. But notice what the psalmist continues to say: "There will I make the horn of David to bud: I have ordained a lamp for mine anointed. His enemies will I clothe with shame: but upon himself shall his crown flourish" (Psalm 132:17,18).

We have reference to the enemies of David's seed being subdued, and also a description of the Lord Jesus Christ as the "horn of David". The horn in scripture is a symbol of strength because the strength of an animal lies in its horns. This descendant of David would be a strong one, because through him salvation would be won for his people.

The dayspring from on high
The psalmist in Psalm 132 looks forward to the time when the horn of David would "bud" in Zion. The Revised Version margin says "spring forth". The word in the Hebrew is *tsamach*, and it is a word that is intimately associated with the covenant made with David.*

It is not coincidence that the corresponding Greek word (*anatole*)** is used by Zacharias in verse 78 of his psalm: "Through the tender mercy of our God; whereby the *dayspring* from on high hath visited us" (Luke 1:78).

The AV margin for "dayspring" has an alternative reading: "sunrising, or branch". This is an interesting

---

* Hebrew: *tsamach*. Gesenius, *Hebrew-Chaldee Lexicon to the Old Testament*: "To sprout forth, used of plants, Genesis 2:5; 41:6. Metaphorically used of the first beginnings of things which occurred in the world, Isaiah 42:9; 43:19; 58:8." In the following references *tsamach* is used in connection with the covenants: 2 Samuel 23:5; Psalm 85:11; 132:11; Isaiah 42:9; 43:19; 45:8; Jeremiah 33:15; Zechariah 6:12.
** Greek: *anatole*. Zodhiates, *The Complete Word Study Dictionary – New Testament*: "The dayspring or dawn, used only in a spiritual sense (Luke 1:78). The word in the singular or the plural also refers to that region or those parts of the heaven or earth where the solar light first springs up and appears, the east, the dayspring, dawn, the rising sun. A shoot." In the Septuagint *anatole* corresponds to the Hebrew *tsamach* in Jeremiah 23:5; Ezekiel 16:7; 17:10; Zechariah 3:8; 6:12.

25

word because in the New Testament it is used in two different, but related, ways. The margin hints at both of them, and both meanings are implicit in what Zacharias was saying:

- First, there is the branch – something that shoots forth, or buds. This is the idea of Psalm 132. The writer to the Hebrews uses the same word in this sense in Hebrews 7:14, when he says that "our Lord sprang out of Judah; of which tribe Moses spake nothing concerning priesthood".

- Secondly, there is the rising of the sun. In the morning the sun appears to spring up, or shoot forth, from the earth. This idea corresponds well with the context in Luke 1, because Zacharias says that the dayspring would "give light to them that sit in darkness and in the shadow of death" (verse 79). This idea is taken from the prophecy of Isaiah: "The people that walked in darkness have seen a great light: they that dwell in the land of the shadow of death, upon them hath the light shined" (Isaiah 9:2). "I the LORD have called thee in righteousness, and will hold thine hand, and will keep thee, and give thee for a covenant of the people, for a light of the Gentiles; to open the blind eyes, to bring out the prisoners from the prison, and them that sit in darkness out of the prison house" (Isaiah 42:6,7). Malachi 4:2 is also relevant, for the prophet speaks of Jesus as the "Sun of righteousness" who will "arise with healing in his wings" (verse 2). The context in Malachi is particularly appropriate to the work of John the Baptist, and the future work of Elijah, as we shall see in due course.

It is evident therefore, that this beautiful psalm of Zacharias is built upon the basis of the covenants made with Abraham and David. These are our covenants, which we have embraced through Christ, the promised seed, and they lie at the very foundation of our faith. The principle of redemption and justification by faith is there in the covenants, and this is where our hope lies.

God manifestation

The doctrine of God manifestation is another of the great themes that run through this psalm. It is God's intention to fill the earth with His glory (Numbers 14:21), and He will do so by means of a multitude of redeemed people who will all reflect His glory and share the divine nature. These redeemed ones are those who, by baptism into Christ, have "put on Christ", and are therefore "Abraham's seed, and heirs according to the promise" (Galatians 3:27-29). There is therefore an association between the covenants of promise and the doctrine of God manifestation – the two are very much intertwined. In many ways they can be considered as the two great pillars upon which the Truth is built. Here, in the Psalm of Zacharias, is just such an example:

"Blessed be the Lord God of Israel; for he hath visited and redeemed his people." (Luke 1:68)

God was visiting His people. How did this take place? God did not literally leave His throne in the heavens – He sent His Son, the Lord Jesus Christ, the seed of Abraham, who was God manifest in the flesh (1 Timothy 3:16). In his life Jesus demonstrated to mankind the character and glory of the Almighty. In effect, he showed us what God is like:

"The Word was made flesh, and dwelt among us, (and we beheld his glory, the glory as of the only begotten of the Father,) full of grace and truth." (John 1:14)

The tragedy was that for the most part this was not appreciated. John's Gospel says that "he came unto his own, and his own received him not" (John 1:11). Nevertheless there were some in Israel who did recognise this, and saw Jesus for who he really was. We have one example in Luke 7, the occasion when Jesus raised the widow's son from the dead at Nain:

"There came a fear on all: and they glorified God, saying, That a great prophet is risen up among us; and, That God hath visited his people. And this

27

rumour of him went forth throughout all Judaea, and
throughout all the region round about."

(Luke 7:16,17)

Through the works that Jesus performed, and the things
that he said, God was visiting His people. This visitation
was for a very specific purpose – to bring redemption and
ultimately salvation from the great enemy of sin and
death. As Zacharias said, God had "visited *and redeemed*
his people ... that we should be saved from our enemies".
This was aptly illustrated by the raising of the widow's
son from the dead.

The prophet of the Highest

It was in order to prepare the way for this divine
visitation that John was sent. And so when Zacharias
speaks about the work of John, he says:

"And thou, child, shalt be called the prophet of the
Highest: for thou shalt go before the face of the Lord to
prepare his ways; to give knowledge of salvation unto
his people by the remission of their sins."

(Luke 1:76,77)

Zacharias says here that John was to be called "the
prophet of *the Highest*". The Revised Version says "most
High". It was for the most High that John was to prepare
the way. Our understanding of God manifestation
enables us to appreciate how this was to be. It is
interesting to observe that in the two major Old
Testament prophecies concerning the work of John the
Baptist – Isaiah 40 and Malachi 3 – this teaching is
present.

Isaiah, for example, says:

"The voice of him that crieth in the wilderness,
Prepare ye the way of *the LORD*, make straight in the
desert a highway for *our God*. Every valley shall be
exalted, and every mountain and hill shall be made
low: and the crooked shall be made straight, and the
rough places plain: and the *glory of the LORD* shall be
revealed, and all flesh shall see it together: for the
mouth of the LORD hath spoken it."   (Isaiah 40:3,5)

John's mission would be to prepare the way for Yahweh, to make a highway for our God, so that His glory might be revealed.

Similarly, in Malachi 3, God declared:

"Behold, I will send my messenger, and he shall prepare the way *before me*: and the Lord, whom ye seek, shall suddenly come to his temple, even the messenger of the covenant, whom ye delight in: behold, he shall come, saith the LORD of hosts."

(Malachi 3:1)

John's ministry was for the purpose of preparing the way before God, because through the person of His Son, the Lord Jesus Christ, God was visiting and redeeming His people, and delivering them from the enemy. No wonder John is styled the greatest of the prophets!

The Exodus

Although God was visiting His people in a unique way, through the person of His only begotten Son, this was not the first time that God had visited and redeemed His people. The Psalm of Zacharias is based upon the events of the Exodus, and a familiarity with the circumstances surrounding this will enlarge our understanding of the greater work of God in visiting His people through Jesus Christ.

Exodus 3 records the incident of the burning bush, when God revealed Himself to Moses, and the memorial name was declared to him with all its meaning. Having revealed Himself to Moses, God commanded Moses to go and speak to the children of Israel:

"Go, and gather the elders of Israel together, and say unto them, The LORD God of your fathers, the God of Abraham, of Isaac, and of Jacob, appeared unto me, saying, *I have surely visited you*, and seen that which is done to you in Egypt: and I have said, I will bring you up out of the affliction of Egypt unto the land of the Canaanites, and the Hittites, and the Amorites, and the Perizzites, and the Hivites, and the Jebusites, unto a land flowing with milk and honey."

(Exodus 3:16,17)

How was this visitation accomplished? It was by manifestation through the angel of the Lord:

"Now Moses kept the flock of Jethro his father in law, the priest of Midian: and he led the flock to the backside of the desert, and came to the mountain of God, even to Horeb. *And the angel of the LORD appeared unto him* in a flame of fire out of the midst of a bush: and he looked, and, behold, the bush burned with fire, and the bush was not consumed."

(Exodus 3:1,2)

It was thus the angel that said to Moses, "I have surely visited you, and seen that which is done to you in Egypt". He was going to redeem them from the land of Egypt.

God again declared His intention to bring them out from under the burdens of the Egyptians, and rid them of their bondage. In this context it is interesting to observe that in Exodus 6 the covenants of promise, the doctrine of God manifestation, and God's visitation to redeem His people, are all combined:

"I appeared unto Abraham, unto Isaac, and unto Jacob, by the name of God Almighty, but by my name Jehovah was I not known to them*. And I have also established *my covenant* with them, to give them the land of Canaan, the land of their pilgrimage, wherein they were strangers ... And I will bring you in unto the

---

* This passage creates an interesting difficulty because it seems to be indicating that the divine name was not known before the incident of the burning bush, and yet in Genesis 15:7 God clearly said to Abraham, "I am the LORD (Yahweh) that brought thee out of Ur of the Chaldees, to give thee this land to inherit it". Similarly, in Genesis 22:14 in the context of the offering up of Isaac on Mount Moriah, "Abraham called the name of that place Jehovah Jireh". The difficulty can be resolved by reading the statement in Exodus 6:3 as a rhetorical question, thus: "I appeared to Abraham, unto Isaac, and unto Jacob by the name of God Almighty, but is it not also true that by my name Yahweh I was known to them?" The answer to the question is emphatically, Yes!

land, concerning the which *I did swear* to give it to Abraham, to Isaac, and to Jacob; and I will give it you for an heritage: *I am the LORD.*" (Exodus 6:3,4,8)

Here we have the things of the name of Yahweh, and all that stands for, intertwined with the covenant made with Abraham. It is in this context that God says:

"Wherefore say unto the children of Israel, I am the LORD, and I will bring you out from under the burdens of the Egyptians, and I will rid you out of their bondage, *and I will redeem you* with a stretched out arm, and with great judgments." (Exodus 6:6)

This is what God did in a most dramatic way. He redeemed Israel out of the iron furnace of Egypt, and at the same time He destroyed the enemy, when the Egyptian hosts were drowned in the Red Sea. He did so, not because the Israelites were any better than any other people, but because of the covenants He had made with Abraham, Isaac and Jacob.

Exodus chapter 15

When this was subsequently accomplished, the children of Israel celebrated their deliverance from the hands of the Egyptians in the words of a song, recorded in Exodus 15. It is interesting to read through this song with the Psalm of Zacharias in mind:

"The LORD is my strength and song, and he is become *my salvation*: he is my God, and I will prepare him an habitation; my father's God, and I will exalt him ... Thy right hand, O LORD, is become glorious in power: thy right hand, O LORD, hath dashed in pieces *the enemy* ... Thou in thy mercy hast led forth the people which thou hast *redeemed*: thou hast guided them in thy strength unto thy holy habitation." (Exodus 15:2,6,13)

In Zacharias' days, God was again about to visit His people Israel. Not this time by manifestation through an angel – but by manifestation through a member of the human race. So it was that, in the fullness of time, God sent forth His Son – made of the seed of David according

31

to the flesh, and made of a woman, made under the law, to redeem them that were under the law. The events of the Exodus were a foretaste of that greater act of redemption secured through Jesus Christ, for whom John was to prepare the way.

We should rejoice that this was accomplished, because through the work of that dayspring from on high, we have been given light, and our feet have been planted in the way of peace. Thus reconciled to God, we have espoused those great and precious promises that have been the theme of this psalm. Through our association with Jesus, we have become Abraham's seed, and heirs according to the promise.

4

THE BAPTISM OF JOHN

OF the childhood and early years of John we know nothing, save for Luke's comment that "the child grew, and waxed strong in spirit, and was in the deserts till the day of his shewing unto Israel" (Luke 1:80). John's early life was a time of growth, both physically and spiritually. Luke's description of John's development resembles that of Samuel (1 Samuel 2:26) and of the Lord himself (Luke 2:40,52). The desert probably refers to the wilderness of Judaea, a region not entirely uninhabited, but well away from the distractions of busy towns and cities. When Luke speaks about "the day of his shewing* unto Israel", he uses a unique Greek word, found nowhere else in scripture, which means 'to exhibit'. He is telling us that when people went out to John, they went to see something, which is why Jesus later asked the question, "What went ye out for to see?" They saw a living example of what John was preaching. Although John was "a voice crying", he was more than that. He put into practice what he preached, and he led by personal example. We shall see this as we continue our analysis of John's life and ministry.

Was John an Essene?

It is sometimes suggested that whilst he was in the desert, John attached himself to an ascetic community known as the Essenes, who inhabited the area of Qumran, where the Dead Sea Scrolls were found. This suggestion is based on the fact that the Essenes placed great emphasis on bathing with water. However, they also held a number of strange beliefs including the

---

* Greek *anadeixis*: to exhibit. It is derived from *anadeiknumi*. Thayer, *Greek-English Lexicon of the New Testament*: "To lift up anything on high and exhibit it for all to behold."

worship of the sun and of angels, the prohibition of marriage, and the practice of magic. They denied the resurrection of the body. They took the observance of the sabbath to such an extreme that they would not even lift a vessel on the sabbath day. They objected to the slaughter of animals, and would have nothing to do with the sacrifices of the Law of Moses. For these reasons we can categorically say that John the Baptist had nothing in common with this sect.*

"The word of God came to John"

Notice how Luke introduces the ministry of John to us, in chapter 3. He focuses on "the day of his shewing unto Israel":

> "Now in the fifteenth year of the reign of Tiberius Caesar, Pontius Pilate being governor of Judaea, and Herod being tetrarch of Galilee, and his brother Philip tetrarch of Ituraea and of the region of Trachonitis, and Lysanias the tetrarch of Abilene, Annas and Caiaphas being the high priests, the word of God came unto John the son of Zacharias in the wilderness."

(verses 1,2)

Luke is very careful to set the ministry of John in its correct historical setting.

Tiberius Caesar

Tiberius was the stepson and successor of Caesar Augustus. He lived until AD 37, and hence was emperor for the entire period of Jesus' ministry. He was a very suspicious man, and hypocritical in his dealings with others. His reign was characterised by a series of murders of close acquain-

---

* For an in depth examination of the Essenes, see J. B. Lightfoot, *St. Paul's Epistles to the Colossians and Philemon*, pages 349-419.

tances. He spent the last ten years of his life on Capri, where he indulged in all manner of sexual perversions. His subjects came to despise him, and after his death the Senate unusually refused to deify him.

Caesar Augustus died in AD 14, and for the last two years of his reign, the sovereignty was shared with Tiberius. This means that the fifteenth year of Tiberius was AD 27, and this represents the commencement of the ministry of John.

It would seem fitting to assume that John commenced his ministry at the age of thirty, the same age that the Levites began active duty (Numbers 4:3). John was six months older than the Lord Jesus Christ, and Luke tells us that Jesus was "about thirty years of age" when he was baptized by John (Luke 3:23). This suggests that the ministry of John prior to the manifestation of the Lord Jesus was comparatively short – little more than six months.

Pontius Pilate

Pilate was appointed the fifth Roman Procurator of Judaea by Tiberias Caesar. He governed for ten years, AD 25-36. His rule thus covered the ministry of the Lord Jesus Christ, and the early years of Christianity in Judaea. His rule was characterised by a series of ill-judged decisions that antagonised the Jews. He was ultimately recalled to Rome, and Eusebius suggests that he committed suicide.

Herod, tetrarch of Galilee

This was Herod Antipas, son of Herod the Great and Malthace. He reigned for forty-two years, his reign concluding in AD 39 when he was banished by Caligula to Lugdunum in Gaul. He ultimately died in Spain. The whole of the ministries of John and the Lord Jesus took place during his rulership.

35

Philip, tetrarch of Iturea and Trachonitis

Herod Philip was the son of Herod the Great and Cleopatra. He reigned for thirty-eight years, concluding in AD 34. Iturea and Trachonitis represented the district to the north and east of the Sea of Galilee. He was different to the other sons of Herod in that he was a moderate and peaceful man.

Lysanias, tetrarch of Abilene

Before the time of John, there was a Lysanias, son and successor of Ptolemy king of Chalcis under Mount Lebanon, and therefore in all probability tetrarch of Abilene. He was assassinated by Antony in 36 BC, who gave part of his dominion to Cleopatra.* Secular history makes no mention of any other Lysanias, but the tetrarch referred to by Luke was probably a descendant of Lysanias, son of Ptolemy.

Annas and Caiaphas the high priests

Annas was deposed by the predecessor of Pilate, Valerius Gratus, in AD 14. Following him, four priestly rulers were chosen and deposed in succession. Caiaphas, the son-in-law of Annas, was appointed by Gratus in AD 17, and he remained in office until AD 36. But under Mosaic law, the office of high priest was held for life (Numbers 35:25), and it was therefore quite legitimate for Luke to call Annas the high priest, even though he had been deposed some years earlier. In reality, Annas continued to hold considerable sway after he was deposed, especially during the high priesthood of his son-in-law Caiaphas. Hence, when Jesus was on trial, he was led away to Annas first, who then sent him to Caiaphas (John 18:13,24).

Why is Luke so anxious to tell us all this historical information? It cannot simply be because he is a careful historian, although undoubtedly he is. The point he is making is that standing alongside the world's great men, every one of them totally corrupt, were the Jewish high

* See F. Josephus, *Antiquities*, xv.4,1.

priests – Annas, and his son-in-law Caiaphas. What a sad situation! The very people who should have been giving the nation of Israel a firm spiritual lead were no better than these corrupt rulers of the age.

But the most telling comment is found at the end of Luke 3:2: "The word of God came unto John the son of Zacharias in the wilderness". The word of God bypassed the high priests in Jerusalem. Instead, God spoke to John in the wilderness.

"All the country about Jordan"

"And he came into all the country about Jordan, preaching the baptism of repentance for the remission of sins" (verse 3). It is an interesting exercise to put together the Gospel accounts, and to see what sort of territory John covered in his preaching. Luke indicates to us here that his early ministry focused on the wilderness of Judaea. Mark confirms for us that John baptized people "in the river of Jordan" (Mark 1:5). Matthew tells us that "there went out to him Jerusalem, and all Judaea, and all the region round about Jordan" (Matthew 3:5), which suggests that he preached along the full length of the Jordan. In fact, John is introduced to us in John 1:28 at "Bethabara beyond Jordan". Nearly all the ancient manuscripts read "Bethany" instead of "Bethabara". It is likely that there was a place called Bethany in the vicinity of the Jordan, which must be distinguished from the city of the same name near Jerusalem. Possibly as a result of the Roman war, the location of this town was lost, and we cannot now be certain where this place was. Nevertheless two days later John is clearly in Galilee, because verse 36 tells us that John saw Jesus and cried, "Behold the Lamb of God", as a result of which Simon and Andrew, who fished on the sea of Galilee, were converted. Jesus was certainly in Galilee the following day when he called Philip (verse 43).

John is next heard of "in Aenon near to Salim" where he baptized because of the abundance of water (John

3:23). The precise location of Aenon is uncertain, but one suggestion is that there is a correspondence with the cities of Shilhim and Ain referred to in Joshua 15:32, which were in the inheritance of the tribe of Judah. This was a region characterised by areas of desert, and it would give greater force to John's explanation that Aenon was a suitable place for John to baptize because there was "much water there".

We know that John ended his days in prison (Luke 3:20). He was able to receive visitors there, and so we can assume that his preaching continued even whilst he was in prison. Josephus tells us that this was in Herod's fortress at Machaerus,* east of the Dead Sea.

We can thus see that the preaching of John took him almost the full length of the country, along the Jordan valley. But in fact the influence of John's preaching extended far beyond the boundaries of Israel. We learn in Acts 18 that the preaching of John had reached Apollos at Alexandria, in Egypt. He was an eloquent man, and mighty in the scriptures; he "spake and taught diligently the things of the Lord, knowing only the baptism of John" (Acts 18:24-28). In Acts 19 we read of a group of believers in Ephesus, in Asia Minor who had been baptized unto John's baptism (Acts 19:1-6). We can thank God too that the preaching of John has reached our ears.

This helps to give us a measure of the greatness of both the man and his message.

John's baptism

Luke tells us that John preached "the baptism of repentance for the remission of sins" (3:3). What was the nature of John's baptism, and its basis?

Whatever view we take of the baptism of John, it must be acknowledged that John baptized people on the basis of direct divine commandment; his baptism had the seal of divine approval:

---

* Josephus *Antiquities*, xviii.5,2.

"And John bare record, saying, I saw the Spirit descending from heaven like a dove, and it abode upon him. And I knew him not: but he that sent me to baptize with water, the same said unto me, Upon whom thou shalt see the Spirit descending, and remaining on him, the same is he which baptizeth with the Holy Spirit." (John 1:32,33)

This is also implied in the question that Jesus asked the Pharisees on one occasion: "The baptism of John, was it from heaven, or of men?" (Mark 11:30) – the implication being of course that it was from heaven.

It is sometimes suggested that the Jews already practised baptismal ceremonies for purification and ceremonial uncleanness, and that John's baptism was but an extension of them.* But there is little evidence that baptism was used for either Jews or proselytes before the first century. Godet, for example, says:

"The rite of baptism, which consisted in the plunging of the body more or less completely into water, was not at this period in use among the Jews, neither for the Jews themselves, for whom the law only prescribed lustrations, nor for proselytes from paganism, to whom, according to the testimony of history, baptism was not applied until after the fall of Jerusalem. The very title Baptist, given to John, sufficiently proves that it was he who introduced this rite."**

What John was doing was entirely new, which is why the official delegation of priests and Levites showed such intense interest in John's activities and interrogated him concerning his baptism: "Why baptizest thou?" (John 1:25). If John's baptism was not new, but merely an extension of the ritual cleansings already practised by the Jews, it would hardly have provoked such attention from the Jewish authorities.

---

* See, for example, A. Barnes, *Barnes on the New Testament*, vol. 1, Matthew & Mark, page 22.
** F. Godet, *Commentary on Luke's Gospel*, vol. 1, page 172.

Further, we have to accept the fact that the baptism of John accomplished "remission of sins" for those who were repentant (Luke 3:3). This can be compared with Peter's declaration on the day of Pentecost, "Repent, and be baptized every one of you in the name of Jesus Christ for the remission of sins" (Acts 2:38). So also Paul recalls the words of Ananias to him on the occasion of his own conversion to Christ: "And now why tarriest thou? arise, and be baptized, and wash away thy sins, calling on the name of the Lord" (Acts 22:16). Thus the benefit ascribed to baptism into Christ is precisely the same as that of John's baptism – the remission of sins. Given that "without shedding of blood (there) is no remission" of sins (Hebrews 9:22), we are led to the conclusion that there was little difference between baptism practised by John and baptism as we know it today. The basis for such remission of sins could only be the sacrifice of Jesus. Just as baptism today points back to the sacrifice of Christ, so John's baptism was pointing forward in time to Jesus' death and resurrection. In fact John's baptism was not in his own name, but he clearly preached Christ crucified, as it were in prospect, when he said that "they should believe on him that should come after him, that is, on Christ Jesus" (Acts 19:4). John proclaimed, "Behold the Lamb of God, which taketh away the sin of the world" (John 1:29).

The baptisms that Jesus himself performed by means of his disciples during his ministry must also be viewed in this light:

"After these things came Jesus and his disciples into the land of Judaea; and there he tarried with them, and baptized. And John also was baptizing in Aenon near to Salim, because there was much water there: and they came, and were baptized."

(John 3:22,23)

This event follows the conversation Jesus had with Nicodemus about being born again. It is difficult to think that what Jesus was doing here before his crucifixion could be any less efficacious than baptisms taking place

40

afterwards. If so, there is no need to view John's baptisms any differently.

Other believers

In Acts 18 we read about Apollos. Here was a man who was "instructed in the way of the Lord; and being fervent in spirit, he spake and taught carefully the things concerning Jesus" (Acts 18:25, RV). He was able to do this purely on the basis of his understanding of John's message – he knew "only the baptism of John". Perhaps because he came from Alexandria in Egypt, he had not yet become acquainted with the fact that Jesus had actually died and risen again. Nevertheless, John's teaching enabled him to preach "the things concerning Jesus".

We do have the case of the believers at Ephesus in Acts 19, who were baptized "unto John's baptism", and yet needed to be baptized again. It is sometimes suggested on the basis of this that these believers were re-baptized into Christ because the baptism of John was inadequate. If this was the case, then it must also be maintained that all former disciples of John had to be re-baptized into Christ. But the fact remains that there is no other instance in the New Testament of the re-baptism of a former disciple of John. Even in the case of Apollos mentioned above, although Aquila and Priscilla "expounded unto him the way of God more perfectly", there is no suggestion that they baptized him before he was accepted into the ecclesia.

Why, then, was it necessary for the believers in Ephesus to be baptized again? It is clear from the record that their understanding of the Gospel was incomplete, because they did not appear to have heard about the Holy Spirit:

"And it came to pass, that, while Apollos was at Corinth, Paul having passed through the upper coasts came to Ephesus: and finding certain disciples, he said unto them, Have ye received the Holy Spirit since ye believed? And they said unto him, We have not so much as heard whether there be any Holy Spirit. And he said unto them, Unto what then were ye baptized? And they said, Unto John's baptism." (Acts 19:1-3)

We have to conclude that they had not even been adequately instructed as disciples of John, because John clearly taught of the coming of the Lord who would baptize with the Holy Spirit and with fire. The strong implication is that they had not been taught first-hand by John, but rather imperfectly by one of John's followers. Had they been properly instructed by John himself, they would have understood about the Holy Spirit. Furthermore, in Paul's comments to the believers at Ephesus that follow, there was nothing new that was not also taught by John: "Then said Paul, John verily baptized with the baptism of repentance, saying unto the people, that they should believe on him which should come after him, that is, on Christ Jesus" (Acts 19:4). It thus seems that the reason why these believers had to be baptized again was not because John's baptism was inadequate, but because their understanding of the Truth at that stage was incomplete.

The baptism of Jesus

The Lord considered it necessary to submit himself to the baptism of John, but if that baptism was little more than an outward token of repentance, why was it necessary for Jesus? The Lord gave the explanation in these words:

"Suffer it to be so now: for thus it becometh us to fulfil all righteousness." (Matthew 3:15)

Jesus' baptism was necessary to "fulfil all righteousness". Luke is very careful to point out in his record that Jesus came *with the others* to John, seeking for baptism, thus emphasising his humanity:

"Now when *all the people* were baptized, it came to pass, that *Jesus also* being baptized, and praying, the heaven was opened." (Luke 3:21)

Here was Jesus, acknowledging the fact that he too was a member of Adam's race, and as such he needed salvation. Whilst he had no sins to be repented of, nevertheless he did need to be saved "out of death" (Hebrews 5:7, RV margin), and that salvation was to be achieved by his own sacrifice. His baptism pointed forward to that: it was an outward symbol of his own death and resurrection, whereby the righteousness of God was declared (Romans 3:26). By submitting to the waters of baptism, he was associating himself with his own sacrifice, and he was acknowledging that he, the great shepherd of the sheep, would be brought again from the dead "through the blood of the everlasting covenant" (Hebrews 13:20).

We conclude therefore that the purpose, meaning and basis of John's baptism were essentially the same as baptism practised today.

The River Jordan –
one of the possible sites of John's baptism

5

THE PREACHING OF JOHN

LUKE introduces his account of the beginning of John's ministry by listing the men who occupied positions of power in the land of Israel at the time. The word of God bypassed them all, and instead it came to John in the wilderness. Matthew simply begins by saying that "in those days came John the Baptist preaching in the wilderness of Judaea, and saying, Repent ye: for the kingdom of heaven is at hand" (Matthew 3:1,2).

The kingdom of heaven is at hand

In what sense could John say that the kingdom of heaven was at hand? Clearly, it was not literally true since the kingdom of God has not yet come, two thousand years after the time of John. John's words must be understood in relation to the advent of the Lord Jesus Christ, the King of the kingdom. His ministry was about to begin, and in his teaching and works he would demonstrate the qualities of the kingdom for all to see. This is how we should understand the words of Jesus himself to the Pharisees, those blind leaders of the blind, who did not recognise him for who he was:

"The kingdom of God is not coming with signs to be observed; nor will they say, 'Lo, here it is!' Or 'There!' for behold, the kingdom of God is in the midst of you."
(Luke 17:20,21, RSV)*

Similarly, it was in this sense that the inhabitants of Jerusalem greeted the Lord as he entered into the city on the colt, believing that Jesus would establish the kingdom there and then:

---

* The Diaglott renders this as follows: "Nor shall they say, 'Behold here! Or there!' for, behold, God's royal majesty is among you."

44

"Hosanna; Blessed is he that cometh in the name of the Lord: blessed be the kingdom of our father David, that cometh in the name of the Lord: Hosanna in the highest."* (Mark 11:9,10)

"The voice of one that crieth"

It is significant that all three synoptic Gospels describe the ministry of John as the fulfilment of Isaiah chapter 40. It is not surprising that since the purpose of John's ministry was to prepare the way for the Messiah, spoken of so frequently in the pages of the Old Testament, so the ministry of John, the greatest of the prophets, should also be prophetically foretold:

"And he came into all the country about Jordan, preaching the baptism of repentance for the remission of sins; as it is written in the book of the words of Esaias the prophet, saying, The voice of one crying in the wilderness, Prepare ye the way of the Lord, make his paths straight. Every valley shall be filled, and every mountain and hill shall be brought low; and the crooked shall be made straight, and the rough ways shall be made smooth; and all flesh shall see the salvation of God." (Luke 3:3-6)

The text literally says, "A voice of one crying!" The construction of the Hebrew in Isaiah 40:3, and the Greek in Luke 3:4, allows for the ensuing phrase, "in the wilderness", to be attached either to what precedes it – "crying in the wilderness" – or to what follows – "prepare ye in the wilderness the way of the Lord". But there is a parallelism present in the verse, which confirms that the correct reading is that adopted by the Revised Version of Isaiah 40:3: "The voice of one that crieth, Prepare ye in the wilderness the way of the LORD, make straight in the desert a high way for our God."

• Prepare ... in the wilderness ... the way of the Lord.

---

* The following references should also be considered in this light: Matthew 10:7; 12:28; Luke 10:9,11; 11:20; 21:31.

45

- Make straight ... in the desert ... a highway for our God.

The image is taken from an oriental custom. The visit of a king would be preceded by the arrival of a courier, who would call upon the people to prepare the road for the arrival of the monarch, by removing the stones and other obstacles out of the way.

This was the purpose of John's mission – to prepare for the Lord's coming, and he was to do so in the wilderness. This does not simply indicate that John's dwelling was in the wilderness of Judaea. It is a commentary on the spiritual barrenness of the nation of Israel in his days. Israel at this time was a spiritual desert, so much so that Isaiah said concerning Jesus that he would "grow up before him as a tender plant, and as a root out of a dry ground" (53:2). This was the sort of spiritual environment in which John had to prepare the way.

The effect of John's preaching

Isaiah continues by describing the effect of John's preaching:

"Every valley shall be exalted, and every mountain and hill shall be made low: and the crooked shall be made straight, and the rough places plain." (40:4)

The prophet is speaking metaphorically; he is describing the effect that John's preaching would have on different types of people:

- The valleys were the common people who were receptive to the word of God. They would be lifted up and given hope.
- The mountains and hills were the proud – people like the scribes and Pharisees who considered themselves superior to others. They were going to be brought down to size.
- The crooked were the crooks – like the publicans who made a living out of defrauding others. They would be straightened out.

- The rough places were the soldiers, who would be smoothed out.

Essentially John's preaching was going to bring everyone down to the same level – the one described by Isaiah 40: "All flesh is grass, and all the goodliness thereof is as the flower of the field" (verse 6). All flesh is grass, and like the grass all will wither and pass away, unless there is repentance from the heart and remission of sins. In contrast, verse 8 says, "The word of our God shall stand for ever". By his teaching, John was preparing the way for Jesus, who was the word made flesh.

When Jesus finally came, all flesh saw "the salvation of God" (Luke 3:6). The phraseology in Isaiah 40 is slightly different: "And the glory of the LORD shall be revealed, and all flesh shall see it together: for the mouth of the LORD hath spoken it" (Isaiah 40:5). The glory of God that was revealed to Moses in the mount (Exodus 34:6,7) would be manifested in the life of the Lord Jesus Christ, to such a degree that John was able to write:

"And the Word was made flesh, and dwelt among us (and we beheld his glory, the glory as of the only begotten of the Father), full of grace and truth … And of his fulness have all we received, and grace for grace. For the law was given by Moses, but grace and truth came by Jesus Christ. No man hath seen God at any time; the only begotten Son, which is in the bosom of the Father, he hath declared him." (John 1:14-18)

The life of grace and truth lived by the Lord Jesus was the means whereby salvation would be brought, not to the Jews only, but to "all flesh", for in Christ Jesus there is neither Jew nor Greek, bond nor free, male nor female (Galatians 3:28).

"Generation of vipers"

The discourse of John, recorded by Matthew and Luke, should not be taken as a particular account of one of John's speeches. Rather it is likely to have been a summary of all John's preaching that was carried out on a number of occasions during his ministry, whilst the

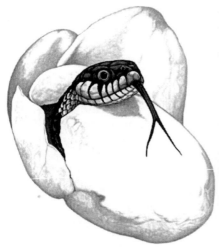

nation was waiting for the coming of the Lord. This is the sense behind Luke 3:7: "Then said he to the multitude that came forth to be baptized of him ..." (Luke 3:7). Literally, "He used to say ..." The burden of his message was that repentance was essential, if judgement was to be avoided:

"Then said he to the multitude that came forth to be baptized of him, O generation of vipers, who hath warned you to flee from the wrath to come? Bring forth therefore fruits worthy of repentance."

(verses 7,8)

Comparing this with Matthew's account, we see that John here was specifically addressing the Pharisees and the Sadducees (Matthew 3:7); they were an offspring of vipers. Jesus described them in a similar way:

"Ye serpents, ye generation of vipers, how can ye escape the damnation of hell?" (23:33)

Perhaps John's words were based upon scenarios that he had observed in the wilderness, where bush fires must have been a fairly common occurrence. As the temperature rose, snakes would emerge with great speed, fleeing from the flames. But from the scriptural perspective, John's castigation of the Pharisees and the Sadducees was based upon Genesis 3:15. They were the seed of the serpent – the children of sin*. This is the true picture that John is painting here. The "wrath to come"

---

* We are very familiar with Genesis 3:15, but sometimes over-familiarity can lead to carelessness in understanding. How often have we heard it said that Jesus, the seed of the woman, would deal the seed of the serpent a fatal wound in the head? Careful

is a reference to the impending judgements of AD 70. Jesus used similar language in his Mount Olivet prophecy concerning the Roman desolation of Jerusalem: "For there shall be great distress in the land, and wrath upon this people" (Luke 21:23). The impending judgement of the wayward nation of Israel is a theme that pervades Luke's account of the ministry of John. He returns to it a verse or two later:

"And now also the axe is laid unto the root of the trees: every tree therefore which bringeth not forth good fruit is hewn down, and cast into the fire."

(Luke 3:9)

The symbolism is not difficult to interpret. The "trees" refer to the nation of Israel, God's vine, and His fig tree. The casting into the furnace represents Israel's destruction in AD 70 because of the nation's inability to bring forth fruit unto God. This is a figure that was used by Jesus on a number of occasions – notably in the Parable of the Fig Tree in the Vineyard in Luke 13, which failed to bring forth fruit. The verdict of the owner was: "Cut it down; why cumbereth it the ground?" (verse 7).

It is interesting to note that John uses the plural word "trees". In the Old Testament, the nation of Israel is described as a vine (Psalm 80:8), a fig tree (Joel 1:12), an olive tree (Jeremiah 11:16), and a cedar (Ezekiel

---

reading and identification of the various parties concerned in the promise will reveal that this is not in fact true.

The serpent is representative of sin, the sting of death (1 Corinthians 15:56). The woman stands for the human race that arose from her by descent. The seed of the serpent represents those who follow the principles of sin in their lives – the Scribes and Pharisees were examples of such. The seed of the woman represents the Lord Jesus Christ, made of a woman, made under the law (Galatians 4:4). There would be enmity between the seed of the woman and the seed of the serpent, and the various confrontations between Jesus and the Pharisees are demonstrative of this. But the woman's seed was to bruise the serpent in the head, and in the process the serpent would bruise the woman's seed in the heel. This was accomplished when the Lord Jesus Christ "put away sin by the sacrifice of himself" (Hebrews 9:26).

17:22,23). Jesus also uses the plural word "trees" in his Mount Olivet Prophecy when describing the barrenness of the nation of Israel immediately prior to the judgements of AD 70:

"Behold the fig tree, and all the trees; when they now shoot forth, ye see and know of your own selves that summer is now nigh at hand."   (Luke 21:29,30)

Comparison with the parallel verse in Matthew 24:32 reveals that the point of Jesus' parable was that "the fig tree and all the trees" were productive of only leaves. Good fruit was conspicuous by its absence:

"Now learn a parable of the fig tree; when his branch is yet tender, and putteth forth leaves, ye know that summer is nigh: so likewise ye, when ye shall see all these things, know that it is near, even at the doors."   (Matthew 24:32,33)

The commandment of John the Baptist to bring forth "fruits meet for repentance" had been disregarded by the nation as a whole. There is no scriptural justification for taking Jesus' reference to "all the trees" as relating to the resurgence of independence among Gentile nations in recent years.

"Fruits meet for repentance"

What was John's message to these vipers?

"Bring forth therefore fruits worthy of repentance, and begin not to say within yourselves, We have Abraham to our father: for I say unto you, That God is able of these stones to raise up children unto Abraham."   (Luke 3:8)

The mountains and hills were being brought low. The Pharisees and Sadducees prided themselves on their ancestry from Abraham, but this was of no consequence in the eyes of God. Just because they had Abraham's blood in their veins did not make them truly the seed of Abraham. In fact, John had already told them they were the seed of the serpent.

On one occasion Jesus said to the Jews, "If ye were Abraham's children, ye would do the works of Abraham … ye are of your father the devil" (John 8:39,44). By their fruits they would be known. Had they truly been Abraham's children, they would have brought forth good fruit. God's purpose has never been worked out on the basis of genealogical descent, because as John said, "God is able of *these stones* to raise up children unto Abraham". It has been suggested that this might refer to the twelve stones erected in Jordan when Israel first entered the Promised Land (Joshua 4:9).

How did the Pharisees respond to these words of rebuke from John? Were their consciences sufficiently pricked for them to confess their sins, and resolve to bring forth fruits meet for repentance? On the contrary, Luke tells us later on in his Gospel that "all the people that heard him, and the publicans, justified God, being baptized with the baptism of John. But the Pharisees and lawyers rejected the counsel of God against themselves, being not baptized of him" (Luke 7:29,30). Not only did they refuse his baptism, they also rejected his teaching, as they themselves admitted when Jesus demanded of them whether the baptism of John was from heaven or of men:

"And they reasoned with themselves, saying, If we shall say, From heaven; he will say unto us, Why did ye not then believe him? But if we shall say, Of men; we fear the people; for all hold John as a prophet."

(Matthew 21:25,26)

Their opinion of John was, "He hath a devil" (Matthew 11:18).

The people

Happily, the people to whom John preached were not all like the Pharisees and Sadducees. There were some among the common people who came to John for the right reasons, with genuine repentance in their hearts. These were the valleys, and they were going to be lifted up by John's teaching:

51

"And the people asked him, saying, What shall we do then? He answereth and saith unto them, He that hath two coats, let him impart to him that hath none; and he that hath meat, let him do likewise."

(Luke 3:10,11)

A spirit of care and compassion for one's fellow men was required, as embodied in the second great commandment of the law: "Thou shalt love thy neighbour as thyself" (Leviticus 19:18). The spirit of John's preaching to the common people finds its way into the later preaching of the apostles, and the lessons are therefore still relevant for us today:

"If a brother or sister be naked, and destitute of daily food, and one of you say unto them, Depart in peace, be ye warmed and filled; notwithstanding ye give them not those things which are needful to the body; what doth it profit? Even so faith, if it hath not works, is dead, being alone." (James 2:15-17)

"But whoso hath this world's good, and seeth his brother have need, and shutteth up his bowels of compassion from him, how dwelleth the love of God in him? My little children, let us not love in word, neither in tongue; but in deed and in truth." (1 John 3:17,18)

John certainly practised what he preached. He was a living embodiment of his message, which was why Jesus asked the Jews, "What went ye out for to see?" John had no material possessions to speak of. He lived in the desert, and everything he wore and ate came from the desert. The irony is that few people would have swallowed their pride sufficiently to accept John's coat of camel skin, if he had offered it to them. Similarly, not many people would have been willing to share a meal of locusts and wild honey with him. It is so easy to let materialism encroach upon our lives and our homes, and crowd out the things that really matter. Where do our priorities lie?

The publicans

"Then came also publicans to be baptized, and said unto him, Master, what shall we do?" (Luke 3:12). The

Romans taxed people by farming out the taxing rights to the highest bidder. The successful man would pay Rome the amount he bid, and collect more than that to pay his expenses and give himself a legitimate profit. However, there was a strong temptation to levy more tax than was strictly necessary and to pocket the extra. Thus the tax collectors became hated in Israel. They were associated by the people with sinners, hence the expression, "publicans and sinners".

But ironically they were amongst the very people who responded to the preaching of the Gospel – Matthew and Zacchaeus, for example. Zacchaeus was from Jericho – right in the heart of John's preaching area. It is an intriguing thought that the seeds of Zacchaeus' repentance might actually have been sown by John the Baptist. Clearly there were others who responded to the teaching of John and came to him for baptism. His message to them was: "Exact no more than that which is appointed you" (Luke 3:13). The crooked were being made straight.

The soldiers
The soldiers mentioned in Luke 3:14 were probably the Jewish zealots – people such as Barabbas who plotted insurrection against Rome. It may be that they were working hand in hand with the tax collectors, providing the necessary backing for them to do their work. But John's message to them was uncompromising: "Do violence to no man, neither exact anything wrongfully; and be content with your wages" (Luke 3:14, RV). They must not take the property of others by unlawful force; neither must they take goods by false accusation. They must be content with the money that was paid them, and also their daily rations. The rough places were made plain.

6

"WHOSE FAN IS IN HIS HAND"

WE have seen how John began his preaching in the wilderness of Judaea, near the Jordan valley, and ascended northwards toward Galilee. By the time we reach Luke 3:15, John is in Galilee. We find the people debating who John really was:

"And as the people were in expectation, and all men mused in their hearts of John, whether he were the Christ, or not ..."

The Authorised Version margin says they were "in suspense".* Daniel's Seventy Weeks prophecy had almost run its course and the time was ripe for the advent of the Messiah.

As far as divine revelation was concerned, there had been a long period of silence. But now this great preacher burst on the scene. How natural therefore for the people to assume that he might be the Messiah. If ever there was an opportunity for John to seize the limelight and to make a name for himself, this was it. But he immediately made it clear that he was not the Messiah:

"John answered, saying unto them all, I indeed baptize you with water; but one mightier than I cometh, the latchet of whose shoes I am not worthy to unloose: he shall baptize you with the Holy Spirit and with fire."   (verse 16)

John was just the forerunner. One mightier than he was coming who would baptize not with water, but with the Holy Spirit and with fire.

---

* "Expectation": Greek, *prosdokao*. Thayer, *Greek-English Lexicon of the New testament*: "To expect (whether in thought, in hope, or in fear); to look for, to wait for".

Baptism of the Holy Spirit

Reference to baptism with the Holy Spirit in the scriptures is quite rare. It is found only in Matthew 3:11, Mark 1:8, John 1:33, Acts 1:5 and 11:16 – all of these involve a comparison with John's baptism. John was prophesying the outpouring of the Holy Spirit gifts upon the early church after the Lord Jesus had been raised from the dead and ascended into heaven. In Acts 1 Jesus commanded his disciples to wait in Jerusalem until they had received the promise of the Holy Spirit, and referred back to the words of John:

> "And [Jesus] being assembled together with them, commanded them that they should not depart from Jerusalem, but wait for the promise of the Father, which, saith he, ye have heard of me. For John truly baptized with water; but ye shall be baptized with the Holy Spirit not many days hence." (Acts 1:4,5)

This was subsequently fulfilled on the day of Pentecost, as Peter explained in Acts 2:

> "This Jesus hath God raised up, whereof we all are witnesses. Therefore being by the right hand of God exalted, and having received of the Father the promise of the Holy Spirit, he hath shed forth this, which ye now see and hear." (Acts 2:32,33)

- Jesus was raised up from the dead.
- He had been exalted to the Father's right hand.
- He had received the promise of the Holy Spirit.
- Jesus had now shed forth the Holy Spirit upon the believers.

The evangelical community lays great emphasis upon the subject of baptism of the Holy Spirit. The words of Jesus are taken by such as applicable to all Christians, not just those who lived in the first century. We must be very clear in our minds that the promise of Jesus was for a particular group of believers at a particular period of time, and for a particular purpose. The belief that baptism of the Holy Spirit is an individual experience for all believers in Christ has no foundation in scripture.

55

Baptism with the Holy Spirit was a corporate experience, and it signified the foundation of the ecclesia in the first century. A comparison can be drawn with the foundation of the nation of Israel in the wilderness by baptism "into Moses in the cloud and in the sea" (1 Corinthians 10:2). As all Israel were baptized in the cloud and in the sea, so the whole ecclesia was baptized with the Holy Spirit, when they were "all with one accord in one place" (Acts 2:1) and they were all filled with the Holy Spirit. That other men received Spirit gifts at other times is clear, but this must not be confused with baptism of the Holy Spirit, which took place at Pentecost.*

Pentecost was primarily a Jewish event. When Peter spoke, he was addressing Jews from every nation under heaven. But in Acts 11, we can see that the Holy Spirit was also subsequently given to Gentiles, again in fulfilment of the words of John the Baptist. Peter again speaks here, rehearsing the events surrounding the baptism of Cornelius:

> "And as I began to speak, the Holy Spirit fell on them, as on us at the beginning. Then remembered I the word of the Lord, how that he said, John indeed baptized with water; but ye shall be baptized with the Holy Spirit. Forasmuch then as God gave them the like gift as he did unto us, who believed on the Lord Jesus Christ; what was I, that I could withstand God? When they heard these things, they held their peace, and glorified God, saying, Then hath God also to the Gentiles granted repentance unto life."
>
> (Acts 11:15-18)

Cornelius and his company of Gentiles received "the like gift" that the Jews had on the day of Pentecost. In effect this event was the Pentecost for the Gentiles, and so in this context reference is made to baptism with the Holy Spirit. Unlike the events on the day of Pentecost,

* For further exposition on this see A. H. Nicholls, *The Evangelical Revival – A Modern Challenge to Biblical Truth*, pages 11-17.

the Holy Spirit was bestowed upon these Gentiles *before* they were baptized. How then could Peter refuse to baptize them with water?

Baptism with fire

Whilst John the Baptist said that the one coming after him would baptize with Holy Spirit and with fire, there is no mention of baptism of the believers with fire, either in Acts 1:5 or Acts 11:16. This is because the baptism of fire had particular significance for *the Jewish nation* that rejected the one for whom John prepared the way. We have seen that one of the themes of John's preaching was the impending judgement of God that would fall on the wayward nation of Israel. They were a spiritual wilderness; they had failed to bring forth fruits meet for repentance, and they were therefore to be judged. The tree was going to be hewn down and cast into the fire.

It was to this act of judgement that John referred when he said to the Jews that the Lord Jesus would baptize them with fire. The Apostle Peter also spoke of this on the day of Pentecost, using Joel's prophecy as his foundation. It is significant that he did so in the context of the outpouring of the Holy Spirit which the Jews had just witnessed:

"For these are not drunken, as ye suppose, seeing it is but the third hour of the day. But this is that which was spoken by the prophet Joel; "And it shall come to pass in the last days, saith God, I will pour out of my Spirit upon all flesh: and your sons and your daughters shall prophesy, and your young men shall see visions, and your old men shall dream dreams: and on my servants and on my handmaidens I will pour out in those days of my Spirit; and they shall prophesy: and I will shew wonders in heaven above, and signs in the earth beneath; blood, *and fire*, and vapour of smoke: the sun shall be turned into darkness, and the moon into blood, before that great and notable day of the Lord come." (Acts 2:15-20)

The people to whom he was speaking had witnessed the baptism of the Holy Spirit. This should have given them the assurance that the baptism of fire would also soon take place – as indeed it did in AD 70, when the Jewish arrangement of things was swept away by the fire of judgement. The prophecy of Joel that Peter quoted began with the words, "And it shall come to pass afterward ...", but Peter purposefully substituted Joel's word "afterward" for "the last days", to emphasise to his audience that Joel's prophecy had specific reference to the last days of Judah's commonwealth, the days in which they lived.*

Peter returned to this subject of impending judgement in his second letter, when he warned the believers that the day of judgement was fast approaching for the nation of Israel:

> "But the day of the Lord will come as a thief in the night; in the which the heavens shall pass away with a great noise, and the elements shall melt with fervent heat, the earth also and the works that are therein shall be burned up." (2 Peter 3:10)

Peter here is not speaking of a future nuclear holocaust, in which the literal heavens and earth will be consumed by fire, because the clear teaching of the scriptures is that the heavens and earth will never be destroyed:

> "Thus saith the LORD, which giveth the sun for a light by day, and the ordinances of the moon and of the stars for a light by night, which divideth the sea when the waves thereof roar; The LORD of hosts is his name: if those ordinances depart from before me, saith the LORD, then the seed of Israel also shall cease from being a nation before me for ever." (Jeremiah 31:35,36)

---

* The following references indicate clearly that it is correct to call the days in which the apostles were living the last days: Hebrews 1:2; James 5:1,3, RV; 1 John 2:18; 2 Peter 3:3 (compare Jude verses 17-19).

"For thus saith the LORD that created the heavens; God himself that formed the earth and made it; he hath established it, he created it not in vain, he formed it to be inhabited: I am the LORD; and there is none else."   (Isaiah 45:18)

Peter's heavens and earth are symbolic, and relate to the nation of Israel in his days,* which was to be destroyed by fire. Even the constituent parts of the Law of Moses, to which the Judaizers in the ecclesia sought to return, were to melt, as Peter said: "The elements shall melt with fervent heat". Peter used a Greek word** that occurs seven times in the New Testament, each time with reference to the elements of the Law of Moses. These elements were emphatically burned up when the temple in Jerusalem, central to the observance of the law, was destroyed.***

Fire unquenchable

John continues his warning of judgement to come:

"Whose fan is in his hand, and he will throughly purge his floor, and will gather the wheat into his garner; but the chaff he will burn with fire unquenchable."   (Luke 3:17)

He is using the symbolism of a harvest. The crops have been reaped, and it is now necessary to separate the wheat from the chaff – the good from the bad. This was done in old time by the use of a long shovel called a fan. The grain was thrown into the air and the wind carried away the chaff, but the good grain fell to the earth. This was gathered safely into the garner, but the chaff was

---

* The same figure of speech is also found in relation to Israel in Deuteronomy 32:1; Isaiah 51:6,13; Daniel 8:10; Joel 2:10,28; 3:15,16; Luke 21:25.

** "Elements": Greek, *stoicheon*. Occurs in Galatians 4:3,9; Colossians 2:8,20; Hebrews 5:12; 2 Peter 3:10,12.

*** For an excellent exposition of 2 Peter 3, see J. Thomas, *The Last Days of Judah's Commonwealth*. Also see J. Allfree, *A World Destroyed by Fire*.

burned up: "The chaff he will burn with *fire unquenchable.*"

This is the language of Gehenna (see Mark 9:43-48), a place of unquenchable fire, that was intimately associated with judgement in times past. Nebuchadnezzar had used the Hinnom Valley as a valley of slaughter during his campaigns against Jerusalem (Jeremiah 7:20,32), and the Romans would put the place to similar use again to dispose of the bodies of the slain. This was why the Lord Jesus said to the Jews: "Ye serpents, ye generation of vipers, how can ye escape the damnation of hell (Gehenna)?" (Matthew 23:33). They were soon to fill up the cup of their iniquity by putting to death the Son of God who came to save them. For this wickedness they would assuredly be judged.

Purge his floor

John said in Luke 3:17 that the Lord Jesus Christ, who would come after him, would "throughly purge his floor". The Revised Version says, "cleanse his threshing-floor". Undoubtedly John is speaking symbolically here, but surely it is no coincidence that the temple, around which the city of Jerusalem was built, was erected on the site of the threshing-floor of Ornan the Jebusite (2 Chronicles 3:1). Here was a sombre warning that the temple would be completely overthrown, so that not one stone would be left standing upon another (Matthew 24:2).

Wheat and chaff

The judgements that were to fall on the nation of Israel, and the city of Jerusalem in particular, would be comprehensive. But there would be opportunity for deliverance for those who heeded the warning signs furnished by the Lord in his Mount Olivet Prophecy. In the terminology of Luke 3:17, the wheat would be safely gathered into the garner. Only the chaff would be burned with fire. The Lord Jesus Christ used very similar language to this in his Parable of the Wheat and the Tares in Matthew 13. Having been told that an enemy had sown tares in his field, the householder issued this order to his servants:

"Let both grow together until the harvest: and in the time of harvest I will say to the reapers, Gather ye together first the tares, and bind them in bundles to burn them: but gather the wheat into my barn."

(13:30)

We can see the similarity with what John said. Whilst it is customary to understand this parable of Jesus in the context of the future judgements of God at the end of the world,* is it not possible that it can be applied to the judgement that befell the nation of Israel in AD 70? The interpretation that Jesus himself gives later on in the chapter, in verses 36-43, would suggest that this is indeed the case:

- The sower of the seed is the Son of man, who preached the Gospel to the nation of Israel during his ministry (13:37).
- The field is the world (13:38). The Greek word is *kosmos*, meaning the ordered arrangement of things. Whilst not exclusively so, *kosmos* is used in the Gospels to refer to the nation of Israel.**
- The good seed are the children of the kingdom (13:38) – people in Jewry who responded to the

* See, for example, J. Carter, *Parables of the Messiah*, pages 92-99.
** G. Kittel, *Theological Dictionary of the New Testament*, vol. 3, page 870: "The kosmos is in the first instance the order whereby the sum of individual things is gathered into a totality. In other words, it is the cosmic system in the sense of the cosmic order ... The world in the special sense, the cosmic system in the sense of the universe". In the symbolic sense, kosmos is frequently used to denote the heavens and earth of Israel's body politic. For examples of this, see John 3:19; 6:14; 7:4; 12:19; 13:1; 15:18; 16:8; 18:20; Romans 1:20; Colossians 2:8,20.

teaching of John and Jesus, and who heeded the warnings of Jesus to "flee into the mountains" at the first sign of Jerusalem's impending destruction (Matthew 24:16).

- The tares are the children of the wicked one (13:38): those who disregarded the warnings of the Lord to their own destruction.

- The enemy that sowed them is the devil (13:39): the scribes and Pharisees, to whom Jesus said, "Ye are of your father the devil, and the lusts of your father ye will do" (John 8:44). These people were directly responsible for the poor spiritual health of the nation, and for the failure of the nation to bring forth fruits meet for repentance. They compassed sea and land to make one proselyte, only to make him twofold more the child of Gehenna than themselves (Matthew 23:15).

- The harvest is the end of the world (13:39). The RV margin says, "the consummation of the age", that is, the Mosaic dispensation. This phrase occurs only six times in the New Testament, and each occurrence relates to the end of the Jewish Age.* It is in this sense that the writer to the Hebrews uses the phrase, when commenting on the sacrifice of the Lord Jesus Christ: "But now once at the end of the ages hath he been manifested to put away sin by the sacrifice of himself" (Hebrews 9:26, RV).

- The reapers are the angels (13:39). It was by means of the "angels" that the Son of man would "gather out of his kingdom all things that offend, and them which do iniquity; and ... cast them into a furnace of fire" (13:41,42). The Greek word simply denotes a messenger,** and in this context represents the

---

* "The end of the world": Greek, *sunteleia aionos*. Found in Matthew 13:39,40,49; 24:3; 28:20; Hebrews 9:26.
** "Angels": Greek, *angelos*. Used of human agencies in Matthew 11:10; 24:31; 25:41; Mark 1:2; 13:27; Luke 7:24,27; 9:52; 2 Corinthians 12:7; James 2:25; 2 Peter 2:4; Jude 6; Revelation 2:1,8,12,18; 3:1,7,14; 12:7.

Roman armies, the medium whereby the baptism of fire was visited upon the workers of iniquity in Israel.

Jesus then says:

"As therefore the tares are gathered and burned in the fire; so shall it be in the end of this world. The Son of man shall send forth his angels, and they shall gather out of his kingdom all things that offend, and them which do iniquity; and shall cast them into a furnace of fire: there shall be wailing and gnashing of teeth." (Matthew 13:40-42)

Thus it came to pass that, in the consummation of the age, when the fiery judgements of God's wrath swept over the nation, those who failed to bring forth fruits meet for repentance were destroyed.

In contrast, the righteous who heeded the words of the Master, and escaped the city of Jerusalem when they saw the judgements approaching, were spared. They are now safely gathered into the garner, and in the future they will be blessed with a place in the kingdom of God: "Then shall the righteous shine forth as the sun in the kingdom of their Father. Who hath ears to hear, let him hear."* (Matthew 13:43)

---

* For further details on this approach to the Parable of the Wheat and the Tares, see J. Thomas, *The Baptism of Fire, The Christadelphian*, vol. 10, 1873, pages 193-202, 241-252.

7

"THIS IS THE RECORD OF JOHN"

IMMEDIATELY after the baptism of the Lord Jesus Christ, the Spirit drove Jesus into the wilderness, where he endured the temptations for forty days (Mark 1:12,13). In the meantime, John continued his ministry, encouraging people to repent in preparation for the manifestation of the Lord.

This is the record of John

It was not long before news of John's activities reached the ears of the Jewish authorities. With some concern for their own authority they embarked upon a fact-finding mission to determine the true motives behind his preaching. John tells us in his Gospel that John the Baptist was interrogated by a delegation of the Jews:

"And this is the record of John, when the Jews sent priests and Levites from Jerusalem to ask him, Who art thou?"
(John 1:19)

The investigation

An official enquiry was taking place here. When John in his Gospel mentions "the Jews", he is referring to the Jewish authorities,* and specifically on many occasions to the Sanhedrin – a senate of seventy-one members, consisting of the chief priests, the elders of the people and the scribes, under the presidency of the high priest. The Revised Version of verse 24 confirms the official nature of this delegation sent to John: "They had been sent from the Pharisees."

One of the divinely given duties of the priests and Levites was that of teaching the laws of God to the people. In the days of Josiah, for example, the Levites

---

* See, for example, John 2:18; 5:10; 7:13; 9:22; 10:24; 18:12,14; 19:7,31; 20:19.

faithfully "taught all Israel" (2 Chronicles 35:3). Malachi the prophet highlighted this responsibility imposed upon the priesthood, whilst at the same time lamenting their failure to discharge that responsibility in his days:

"For the priest's lips should keep knowledge, and they should seek the law at his mouth: for he is the messenger of the LORD of hosts. But ye are departed out of the way; ye have caused many to stumble at the law; ye have corrupted the covenant of Levi, saith the LORD of hosts." (Malachi 2:7,8)

Part of this duty of teaching involved investigating the validity of the claims of teachers and prophets that arose in Israel from time to time, so that they might make a pronouncement concerning them for the guidance of the people. This was legislated for in the Law of Moses:

"And if thou say in thine heart, How shall we know the word which the LORD hath not spoken? When a prophet speaketh in the name of the LORD, if the thing follow not, nor come to pass, that is the thing which the LORD hath not spoken, but the prophet hath spoken it presumptuously: thou shalt not be afraid of him." (Deuteronomy 18:21,22)

Note in passing that this commandment was given in the context of God's promise to raise up a true prophet like unto Moses:

"I will raise them up a Prophet from among their brethren, like unto thee, and will put my words in his mouth; and he shall speak unto them all that I shall command him." (verse 18)

When John first stood on the banks of the Jordan and claimed to speak with the authority of God, it marked the end of four hundred years of silence. The sun had long since gone down over the prophets (Micah 3:6). The authorities would thus have had a particular interest in establishing the validity of John's claim to be a prophet sent from God, and in particular in establishing whether he might be the promised Messiah who was imminently expected, or the prophet like unto Moses predicted of old.

This is what was taking place in John 1. The Jews sent priests and Levites to John to ask him, "Who art thou?" Notice how John replies: "And he confessed, and denied not; but confessed, *I am not the Christ*" (verse 20). Their question was emphatically answered in the negative. The questioning continued: "Art thou Elias?" Again came the emphatic negative from John, "I am not". "Art thou that prophet?" (that is, the prophet like unto Moses of Deuteronomy 18). Answer, "No".

Not satisfied with these denials, the Jews pressed John further for positive identification:

> "Then said they unto him, Who art thou? that we may give an answer to them that sent us. What sayest thou of thyself?" (verse 22)

John's reply was a testimony to the humility of the man. He was nothing more than a voice:

> "He said, I am the voice of one crying in the wilderness, Make straight the way of the Lord, as said the prophet Esaias." (verse 23)

The wilderness

John was making a quotation from Isaiah 40. If they would receive it, this was where John's authority came from – his ministry was foretold by no less than the prophet Isaiah, speaking by inspiration of God. But that same Old Testament prophecy hinted that the Jews would reject John's teaching, because in spiritual terms they were a barren desolate wilderness. The theme of the wilderness is one that recurs through Isaiah's prophecy , and there is a particularly interesting reference in Isaiah 43, because that chapter contains another prophecy concerning the work of John the Baptist.

In Isaiah 43:18 the prophet Isaiah says:

> "Remember ye not the former things, neither consider the things of old. Behold, I will do a new thing; now it shall spring forth; shall ye not know it?" (verses 18,19)

This is speaking about the passing away of the Old Covenant, and its replacement with the New – a transition that was heralded by the ministry of John. "The law and the prophets were until John: since that time the kingdom of God is preached", said Jesus (Luke 16:16).

Isaiah says that this "new thing" would "spring forth".* This would be accomplished through the advent of the Lord Jesus Christ, described by Zacharias, the father of John the Baptist, as "the dayspring from on high" (Luke 1:78). He was the horn who would be made to "spring forth unto David" (Psalm 132:17, RV margin). Through him the New Covenant would be established in fulfilment of the previous chapter of Isaiah:

"I the LORD have called thee in righteousness, and will hold thine hand, and will keep thee, and give thee for a covenant of the people, for a light of the Gentiles … behold, the former things are come to pass, and new things do I declare: before they spring forth I tell you of them."   (Isaiah 42:6-9)

All this was to be heralded by the preaching of John, who would prepare in the wilderness a way for the Lord. Isaiah makes it clear that the work of John had divine authority because it is God, the Holy One of Israel, who says in Isaiah 43:19, "I will even make a way in the wilderness, and rivers in the desert". Not only was John engaged in the work of God, but the one for whom he was preparing the way was none other than God manifest in the flesh. In the words of chapter 40, John was to "prepare in the wilderness the way of the LORD".

What sort of response would be offered to the preaching of John? In Isaiah we read:

"The beast of the field shall honour me, the dragons and the owls: because I give waters in the wilderness, and rivers in the desert, to give drink to my people, my chosen. This people have I formed for myself; they

---

* Hebrew, *tsamach*. See previous comments on page 25 and footnote.

shall shew forth my praise. But thou hast not called upon me, O Jacob; but thou hast been weary of me, O Israel." (43:20-22)

The beasts of the field, the dragons and the owls, unclean creatures according to the law of Leviticus 11, represent the Gentiles. These would receive the Gospel and embrace it; but not so the Jews, who were wearied by it. This willing response of the Gentiles is hinted at in Isaiah 40: "And the glory of the LORD shall be revealed, and *all flesh* shall see it together: for the mouth of the LORD hath spoken it" (verse 5).

What then of Israel? Has God cast away His people (Romans 11:1) for their poor response to the preaching of John and his successor? The Apostle Paul leaves us in no doubt that this is not so, because he says that ultimately "all Israel shall be saved: as it is written, There shall come out of Sion the Deliverer, and shall turn away ungodliness from Jacob: for this is my covenant unto them, when I shall take away their sins" (Romans 11:26,27). Under the terms of the New Covenant that would spring forth, Israel's sins will be forgiven. Isaiah 43 therefore concludes by looking to that future day when Israel will turn to God, and He will blot out all their transgressions: "I, even I, am he that blotteth out thy transgressions for mine own sake, and will not remember thy sins" (verse 25). The day will come when Israel will no longer be a wilderness. It is to this day that the prophet Isaiah looks forward in chapter 35:

"The wilderness and the solitary place (RV margin, parched land) shall be glad for them; and the desert shall rejoice, and blossom as the rose. It shall blossom abundantly, and rejoice even with joy and singing: the glory of Lebanon shall be given unto it, the excellency of Carmel and Sharon, they shall see the glory of the LORD, and the excellency of our God." (verses 1,2)

When Jesus first came, he came as "a root out of a dry ground" (53:2): Israel were spiritually barren and desolate. Although God was visiting His people, and the glory of the Lord was being revealed, the people failed to appreciate it. "He came unto his own, and his own received him not" (John 1:11). But when they look upon him whom they pierced, and mourn for him (Zechariah 12:10), and turn to God in faith and repentance, God will make an everlasting covenant of peace with them, and will place them in their own land with His sanctuary in the midst of them for evermore (Ezekiel 37:26). At long last the wilderness of Israel will blossom abundantly, both literally and symbolically, and Israel shall see the glory of the Lord, and the excellency of our God. In that day, "they shall say, This land that was desolate is become like the garden of Eden; and the waste and desolate and ruined cities are become fenced, and are inhabited" (Ezekiel 36:35).

"For the LORD shall comfort Zion: he will comfort all her waste places; and he will make her wilderness like Eden, and her desert like the garden of the LORD; joy and gladness shall be found therein, thanksgiving, and the voice of melody."   (Isaiah 51:3)

John's first testimony concerning Jesus

Having interrogated John concerning his identity and his authority, the Jewish rulers continued to question him about his baptism: "And they asked him, and said unto him, Why baptizest thou then, if thou be not that Christ, nor Elias, neither that prophet?" (John 1:25). John's reply was the first of three testimonies concerning Jesus that he made to the Jews on three consecutive days. In this first testimony he declared that his baptism was but a preparation for the manifestation of the Messiah, who would be much greater than he:

"John answered them, saying, I baptize with water: but there standeth one among you, whom ye know not; he it is, who coming after me is preferred before me, whose shoe's latchet I am not worthy to unloose."

(verses 26,27)

To unloose a person's shoe-latchet was amongst the humblest of offices performed by slaves. This was John's estimation of his own worth when compared with the Son of God.

John's Gospel narrative does not tell us what conclusions the Jewish deputation drew concerning John and his activities. But we know from elsewhere that they decided that his preaching was not of God. They "rejected the counsel of God against themselves, being not baptized of him" (Luke 7:30). On their own admission, they did not believe John, but were afraid to say so publicly because of the people (Matthew 21:25,26). We also know that the common people drew a different conclusion: they counted John as a prophet.

John's second testimony concerning Jesus

This official interrogation of John took place in Bethabara beyond Jordan, where John was baptizing. The following day John saw Jesus coming towards him, and this provoked John to make his second testimony concerning the Lord, recorded in John 1:29-34. It is very likely that this day marked the end of Jesus' temptations in the wilderness, and the beginning of his ministry amongst the people. We may well imagine that, after such a gruelling experience, the Lord would have had a very distinctive appearance, and this would serve only to draw even greater attention to John's exclamation as he gestured towards Jesus and cried, "Behold the Lamb of God which taketh away the sin of the world" (verse 29).

"Behold the Lamb of God"

Everyone that heard this great pronouncement of John's would have been familiar with the rich symbolism associated with the lamb. It spoke of affection and love (2 Samuel 12:3), but especially of submission and sacrifice. John clearly foresaw that the ultimate purpose of the ministry of the Lord Jesus was to lay down his life as a sacrifice for sin. The Old Testament basis for John's testimony can be traced all the way back to the book of Genesis. After Adam and Eve fell from grace in Eden, the record says that "unto Adam also and to his wife did the LORD God make coats of skins, and clothed them"

(Genesis 3:21), and this covering for their sins clearly required sacrifice. Whilst we cannot be sure that this was a sacrificial lamb, there was nevertheless established a principle that "without shedding of blood is no remission" of sins (Hebrews 9:22). Here was a principle that Abel came to understand, but Cain his brother did not, for "in process of time it came to pass, that Cain brought of the fruit of the ground an offering unto the LORD. And Abel, he also brought of the firstlings of his flock and of the fat thereof. And the LORD had respect unto Abel and to his offering: but unto Cain and to his offering he had not respect" (Genesis 4:3-5).

When God commanded Abraham to offer up Isaac on Mount Moriah for a burnt offering, Abraham the faithful clearly grasped the prophetic significance of the events in which he was caught up. He foresaw the advent of the Lamb of God when he declared to Isaac, "My son, God will provide himself a lamb for a burnt offering" (Genesis 22:8), and this was memorialised in the name that Abraham chose to give to that place: "And Abraham called the name of that place Jehovah-jireh: as it is said to this day, In the mount of the LORD it shall be provided" (verse 14, RV). The marginal note in the Revised Version adds an extra dimension to the name: "In the mount of the LORD he shall be seen". Was this scripture in John's mind as he lifted up his voice and cried, "Behold the Lamb of God"?

When the Law of Moses was subsequently instituted, the lamb had a very prominent role to play in the ritual. There was the daily, continual morning and evening sacrifice, consisting of "two lambs of the first year day by day continually" (Exodus 29:38), which spoke of total dedication to God. To commemorate their deliverance and redemption from Egypt they had to observe the feast of the Passover, and that special meal consisted of a lamb "without blemish, a male of the first year" (Exodus 12:5). The Apostle Peter confirms that this pointed forwards to the greater act of redemption secured by the sacrifice of the Lord Jesus Christ:

"Forasmuch as ye know that ye were not redeemed with corruptible things, as silver and gold, from your vain conversation received by tradition from your fathers; but with the precious blood of Christ, as of a lamb without blemish and without spot."

(1 Peter 1:18,19)

It is perhaps surprising that under the Mosaic dispensation the law of the sin offering had no provision for the offering of a male lamb. The sin offering had to consist of either a young bullock, a male or female kid of the goats, or a female lamb, all of them without blemish (Leviticus 4:3,14,23,28,32). But on reflection there is a wonderful appropriateness to this, because the absence of the male lamb in the ritual of the sin offering served to emphasise that the Lord Jesus Christ – the Lamb of God – was able to take away sin in a way that was not possible under the jurisdiction of the law. This was foreseen in graphic terms by the prophet Isaiah when he spoke of the suffering Servant:

"But he was wounded for our transgressions, he was bruised for our iniquities: the chastisement of our peace was upon him; and with his stripes we are healed. All we like sheep have gone astray; we have turned every one to his own way; and the Lord hath laid on him the iniquity of us all. He was oppressed, and he was afflicted, yet he opened not his mouth: he is brought as a lamb to the slaughter." (Isaiah 53:5-7)

It is significant that it was at this same scripture that Philip the evangelist began to preach Jesus Christ to the eunuch (Acts 8:32-35).

The theme of Jesus Christ as the Lamb of God is developed in the New Testament and it reaches its climax in the book of Revelation, where no less than twenty-seven times Jesus is represented as "a Lamb as it had been slain" whereby redemption has been secured through his blood (Revelation 5:6,9). Because the sacrifice of Jesus was the fulfilment of all the Old Testament types and shadows associated with the lamb, he is described in Revelation 13:8 as "the Lamb slain from the foundation of the world". The sacrifice of Christ was in God's plan right from the beginning, and it was in this sense that John the Baptist was able to say concerning the Lamb of God, "After me cometh a man which is preferred before me, for he was before me" (John 1:30). Whilst Jesus was younger than John by some six months, he was "before" him because he "verily was foreordained before the foundation of the world, but was manifest in these last times for you" (1 Peter 1:20).

Not only was Jesus the Lamb of God, he was also "God … manifest in the flesh" (1 Timothy 3:16). By means of the words he spoke, and the deeds he performed, the character and glory of the Father were exhibited. Whilst it is true that "no man hath seen God at any time", it was equally true that "the only begotten Son, which is in the bosom of the Father, he hath declared him" (John 1:18). John's mission was thus to prepare the way, not for a mere man of human parentage, but for Yahweh in manifestation. John could therefore rightly say, "After me cometh a man which is preferred before me, for he was before me" (verse 30).

"I knew him not"

Twice in his second testimony, John acknowledged that before the occasion of Jesus' baptism, John "knew him not" (John 1:31,33). This might seem somewhat surprising, especially in view of their close family relationship. But this was presumably because they lived some distance apart, and John spent his formative years in the wilderness until "the day of his shewing unto

73

Israel" (Luke 1:80). This being the case, how was John able to recognise Jesus for who he was when Jesus came to him requesting baptism? The answer probably lies in the fact that, when Jesus first presented himself before John, unlike the other people who "were baptized of him in Jordan, confessing their sins" (Matthew 3:6), Jesus had no sins to confess. Endowed as he was with the Spirit of God from his mother's womb, John would be able to see into the heart of the man standing before him, and would appreciate that he was truly in the presence of a sinless man.

John was also given a sign that would confirm without doubt that he had baptized the Messiah:

> "And John bare record, saying, I saw the Spirit descending from heaven like a dove, and it abode upon him. And I knew him not: but he that sent me to baptize with water, the same said unto me, Upon whom thou shalt see the Spirit descending, and remaining on him, the same is he which baptizeth with the Holy Spirit. And I saw, and bare record that this is the Son of God." (John 1:32-34)

Thus it was that "Jesus also being baptized, and praying, the heaven was opened, and the Holy Spirit descended in a bodily shape like a dove upon him, and a voice came from heaven, which said, Thou art my beloved Son; in thee I am well pleased" (Luke 3:21,22). In this way, John had witnessed the fulfilment of prophecy, because in anticipation of this event God had spoken through Isaiah:

> "Behold my servant, whom I uphold; mine elect, in whom my soul delighteth; I have put my spirit upon him: he shall bring forth judgment to the Gentiles."
> (Isaiah 42:1)

John's third testimony concerning Jesus

John's third testimony concerning the Lord took place the day following, whilst he was in the company of two of his disciples:

"Again the next day after John stood, and two of his disciples; and looking upon Jesus as he walked, he saith, Behold the Lamb of God! And the two disciples heard him speak, and they followed Jesus."

(John 1:35-37)

John and his disciples were standing, whilst Jesus was walking. John's words were an invitation to his disciples now to follow the Lord instead. It was the beginning of the process whereby Jesus would increase whilst John would decrease (John 3:30). This invitation was heeded by Andrew, and another unnamed disciple, suggesting quite strongly that it was in fact John himself, the Gospel writer. John 1:41 tells us that "(Andrew) first findeth his own brother Simon", implying that John secondly went to find his brother James.

The following day, Jesus and his small group of disciples were joined by two others: "The day following Jesus would go forth into Galilee, and findeth Philip, and saith unto him, Follow me" (John 1:43). Philip then went to find Nathanael – probably another name for Bartholomew:

"Philip findeth Nathanael, and saith unto him, We have found him, of whom Moses in the law, and the prophets, did write, Jesus of Nazareth, the son of Joseph. And Nathanael said unto him, Can there any good thing come out of Nazareth? Philip saith unto him, Come and see." (John 1:45,46)

Nathanael at first was sceptical about Philip's claim to have found the Messiah, but he was convinced by Jesus' greeting: "Behold an Israelite indeed, in whom is no guile!" (John 1:47).

By the end of John 1, Jesus was thus accompanied by six of his disciples, at least two of whom were disciples of John. Chapter 2 commences by saying: "The *third day* there was a marriage in Cana of Galilee; and the mother of Jesus was there: and both Jesus was called, and his disciples, to the marriage" (verses 1,2). This was now seven days after John the Baptist declared openly that he was not the Christ, but that one greater than he was coming. Whose marriage it was we are not told, but it was the occasion when Jesus turned the water into wine. By so doing, he "manifested forth his glory; and his disciples believed on him" (verse 11).

The question about purifying

We next meet John the Baptist in John 3, where he was "baptizing in Aenon near to Salim, because there was much water there: and they came, and were baptized" (verse 23). Whilst he was baptizing, someone raised a question about purifying. The Revised Version gives the correct sense: "There arose therefore a questioning on the part of John's disciples with a Jew about purifying" (verse 25). This debate was provoked by one particular Jew. Remembering how John in his Gospel uses the phrase "the Jews" to represent those in authority, it seems there was a deliberate attempt by one particular Jewish authority to discredit John in front of his own disciples. Perhaps he was casting doubt upon the benefits of John's baptism by drawing attention to the fact that Jesus baptized people too, and appeared to be growing in popularity.

Thus the seeds of doubt were being sown by this man into the hearts and minds of John's disciples. It seemed to work because John's disciples came to him and asked him about Jesus, and the tone of their remarks gives the impression that they did not altogether approve of the activities of Jesus:

"And they came unto John, and said unto him, Rabbi, he that was with thee beyond Jordan, to whom thou barest witness, behold, the same baptizeth, and all men come to him." (verse 26)

Their question was really a thinly veiled criticism of Jesus for taking over John's role as the Baptist. John responded with characteristic humility:

"A man can receive nothing, except it be given him from heaven. Ye yourselves bear me witness, that I said, I am not the Christ, but that I am sent before him. He that hath the bride is the bridegroom: but the friend of the bridegroom, which standeth and heareth him, rejoiceth greatly because of the bridegroom's voice: this my joy therefore is fulfilled." (verses 27-29)

It is not a coincidence that John uses the symbolism of a wedding in his reply, for only three days before Jesus and his disciples had been to a wedding, and on that occasion Jesus had "manifested forth his glory" (2:11). The news of what Jesus had done at the wedding would have travelled far, and had probably reached the ears of John's disciples. They should have understood that Jesus was the one for whom John was preparing the way, and John continued to emphasise this with a wedding parable. Jesus was the bridegroom, the disciples of Jesus were the bride, and John the Baptist was merely the friend of the bridegroom, whose duty it was to bring bride and groom together. As far as John was concerned, the fact that his disciples were now following Jesus was in fact a cause for joy, not resentment: "This my joy therefore is fulfilled". John knew that "He must increase, but I must decrease" (3:30).

The figure of the bride and the bridegroom should have been known to John's disciples, for it was used by the Old Testament prophets to illustrate God's relationship with His people Israel (Isaiah 54:5; Jeremiah 3:14; Hosea 2:2,19,20). The figure is carried over into the New Testament, the ecclesia being represented as the bride of Christ (Ephesians 5:25,32; Revelation 19:7; 21:9).

A burning and shining light

This is the last public statement from the lips of John. The next time we meet him, he is in prison. But with John's last words in mind, it is interesting to see how Jesus describes John: "He was a burning and a shining light:* and ye were willing for a season to rejoice in his light" (John 5:35). The Greek here signifies a portable lamp that provided light by the burning of oil. When such a lamp was first lit, there would be a brilliant flare of light, but as the oil was consumed it would slowly die out.

This was a perfect description of the ministry of John. He burst on the scene, illuminating all that came into his path. But then when Jesus, "the true Light,** which lighteth every man" (John 1:9) came into the world, John's mission was accomplished, and he slowly receded into the background: "He must increase, but I must decrease."

---

* "Light". Greek, *luchnos*. W. E. Vine, *Expository Dictionary of New Testament Words*: "A portable lamp usually set on a stand".
** "Light". Greek, *phos*. H. Balz and G. Schneider, *Exegetical Dictionary of the New Testament*: "Light; radiance; fire; lamp".

8

JOHN'S IMPRISONMENT

IT is likely that John began his public ministry when he was thirty years of age, in which case it was six months later when he proclaimed, "Behold the Lamb of God that taketh away the sin of the world". It was only a short while after that – some three months or so – when the light of John's ministry was abruptly extinguished by Herod Antipas:

> "And many other things in his exhortation preached he unto the people. But Herod the tetrarch, being reproved by him for Herodias his brother Philip's wife, and for all the evils which Herod had done, added yet this above all, that he shut up John in prison."
>
> (Luke 3:18-20)

Herod Antipas was the son of Herod the Great, and his evil deeds were comparable to those of his father. He ruled from 4 BC to AD 39, so the ministries of both John and Jesus Christ were conducted entirely during his reign. Antipas was essentially a weak and selfish ruler and his private life was steeped in scandal. The Lord's assessment of Herod is to be found in Luke 13:

> "The same day there came certain of the Pharisees, saying unto him, Get thee out, and depart hence: for Herod will kill thee. And he said unto them, Go ye, and tell that fox, Behold, I cast out devils, and I do cures to day and to morrow, and the third day I shall be perfected." (verses 31,32)

The word that Jesus chose to use is of the feminine gender – perhaps this is an indication that the real power behind the throne was Herodias, the wife of Herod Antipas.

Josephus comments on John's imprisonment by Herod, as follows:

"Now, when many others came to crowd about (John), for they were greatly moved by hearing his words, Herod, who feared lest the great influence John had over the people might put it into his power and inclination to raise a rebellion (for they seemed ready to do anything he should advise), thought it best, by putting him to death, to prevent any mischief he might cause, and not bring himself into difficulties, by sparing a man who might make him repent of it when it should be too late. Accordingly he was sent a prisoner, out of Herod's suspicious temper, to Machaerus ... and was there put to death."*

John's preaching no doubt would have come to the ears of Herod, who had probably sent out spies to determine whether John posed a threat to his authority and to the stability of the dominion. But the scriptures tell us that the real reason for John's imprisonment was to do with the matter of Herodias, who was the wife of Herod Philip, the son of Herod the Great by Mariamne, and half brother to Herod Antipas. Herod Antipas had previously married the daughter of Aretas, the Nabatean king of Petra, a marriage that had political motivations, being an attempt to safeguard the Peraean frontier. But on a visit to Rome as guest of Herod Philip, Antipas became infatuated with Herodias, and he lured her away. She agreed to desert Philip and marry him, on condition that he divorce the daughter of Aretas. This he duly did, and when she returned to her father this provoked an ongoing quarrel between the two monarchs, resulting years later in a war in which Herod Antipas suffered a heavy defeat.

There is a hint in Jesus' discussion with the disciples concerning the coming of Elijah that the Jewish authorities had also been involved in encouraging Herod to imprison John:

"And Jesus answered and said unto them, Elias truly shall first come, and restore all things. But I say

---

* Josephus, *Antiquities of the Jews*, xviii.5,2.

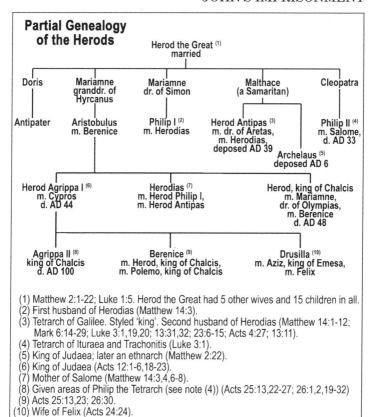

Partial Genealogy of the Herods

(1) Matthew 2:1-22; Luke 1:5. Herod the Great had 5 other wives and 15 children in all.
(2) First husband of Herodias (Matthew 14:3).
(3) Tetrarch of Galilee. Styled 'king'. Second husband of Herodias (Matthew 14:1-12; Mark 6:14-29; Luke 3:1,19,20; 13:31,32; 23:6-15; Acts 4:27; 13:11).
(4) Tetrarch of Ituraea and Trachonitis (Luke 3:1).
(5) King of Judaea; later an ethnarch (Matthew 2:22).
(6) King of Judaea (Acts 12:1-6,18-23).
(7) Mother of Salome (Matthew 14:3,4,6-8).
(8) Given areas of Philip the Tetrarch (see note (4)) (Acts 25:13,22-27; 26:1,2,19-32)
(9) Acts 25:13,23; 26:30.
(10) Wife of Felix (Acts 24:24).

unto you, That Elias is come already, and they knew him not, but have done unto him whatsoever they listed. Likewise shall also the Son of man suffer of them. Then the disciples understood that he spake unto them of John the Baptist." (Matthew 17:11-13) Just as the Lord Jesus Christ himself was to suffer at the hands of the Jews, those same Jews had done to John "whatsoever they listed". Perhaps they had questioned John on his views concerning the marriage between Antipas and Herodias, and sent informers into Herod's court. Whilst this is an assumption, it is entirely reasonable because the subject of marriage and divorce was used by the Jewish authorities on a later occasion to attempt to discredit the Lord Jesus Christ himself (Matthew 19:3-9).

John was uncompromising in his criticism of Herod. Mark in his account tells us that "John had said unto Herod, It is not lawful for thee to have thy brother's wife" (6:18). Under what circumstances John had met Herod we are not told, but the tense of the verb used by Mark indicates that John had said this to Herod on more than one occasion – he kept on saying it. No doubt he would have appealed to the following passages in support of his rebuke:

"Thou shalt not uncover the nakedness of thy brother's wife: it is thy brother's nakedness."

(Leviticus 18:16)

"And if a man shall take his brother's wife, it is an unclean thing: he hath uncovered his brother's nakedness; they shall be childless." (Leviticus 20:21)

Mark indicates that there was some considerable tension between Herod and Herodias over the way John should be treated:

"Therefore Herodias had a quarrel against him, and would have killed him; but she could not: for Herod feared John, knowing that he was a just man and an holy, and observed him (kept him safe, RV); and when he heard him, he did many things, and heard him gladly." (6:19,20)

Herodias wanted John dead – and but for Herod's intervention she would have succeeded earlier than she did. Clearly Herodias had a vested interest in preserving her position in Herod's court, for had Herod expelled her she would have had nowhere to go.

John and Elijah

There is a remarkable parallel here between John and Elijah the prophet:

- John came "in the spirit and power of Elias". Concerning John, Jesus said: "If ye will receive him, this is Elias which was for to come."
- Elijah's arch enemy was wicked king Ahab. But he was very much dominated by his evil scheming wife Jezebel, who vowed to kill Elijah. "And Ahab told Jezebel all that Elijah had done, and withal how he had slain all the prophets with the sword. Then Jezebel sent a messenger unto Elijah, saying, So let the gods do to me, and more also, if I make not thy life as the life of one of them by to morrow about this time" (1 Kings 19:1,2).
- Likewise John ultimately lost his life at the hands of another evil scheming woman, Herodias, who was easily the equal of Jezebel.

Paradoxically, Herod seemed to have a respect for John. Whilst clearly John had no fear of Herod, and did not shrink from highlighting Herod's adultery, Herod "feared John, knowing that he was a just man and an holy, and observed him". The Revised Version indicates that he "kept him safe" (Mark 6:19,20). There was something in Herod that was attracted to the Gospel, and so John was protected from Herodias, and from time to time John was brought up from the dungeon for a personal audience with Herod. He "heard him gladly", and the imperfect tense again implies that these meetings took place repeatedly. Perhaps Herod thought that with repeated discussions with John, a compromise could be worked out with respect to Herodias.

There is an interesting parallel with the Apostle Paul's experiences at the hands of Felix. Felix was originally a slave, and he was elevated to power by the Emperor Claudius. Like Herod Antipas, he was a morally corrupt man, and indulged in all manner of lusts and cruelty. The correspondence with Antipas is remarkable, because Felix became besotted with Drusilla, a daughter of Herod Agrippa I, who was already married. He employed a magician named Simon to use his arts to persuade Drusilla to leave her husband

and marry him, promising that if she would comply he would make her a happy woman. Thus Drusilla became Felix's third wife. The Apostle Paul's experience at the hands of this man was similar to that of John, for he too was unjustly imprisoned because Felix was "willing to shew the Jews a pleasure" (Acts 24:27). But as with Herod Antipas, there was something in Felix that was attracted to the Gospel, and so "after certain days, when Felix came with his wife Drusilla, which was a Jewess, he sent for Paul, and heard him concerning the faith in Christ" (verse 24). Never one to miss an opportunity to preach, Paul reasoned with Felix of "righteousness, temperance, and judgment to come" (verse 25). No doubt John also would have taken the opportunity to preach the Gospel to Herod, and perhaps "righteousness, temperance and judgment to come" was also the substance of his message.

When Paul spoke to Felix of judgement to come, "Felix trembled, and answered, Go thy way for this time; when I have a convenient season, I will call for thee". Likewise, "Herod feared John, knowing that he was a just man and an holy". But in spite of his interest in John's teaching, Herod was unable to commit himself fully to the Truth. Clearly the preaching of John had an impact upon his life, for "when he heard him, he did many things, and heard him gladly" (Mark 6:20). But one thing was necessary, and Herod was not prepared to do that, for he was not able to stand up to his wife. In the terms of Jesus' Parable of the Sower, Herod was an example of thorny ground, in which "cares and riches and pleasures of this life" choked the word, that it became unfruitful. Unfortunately for Herod, the opportunity to bring forth fruits meet for repentance came and went.

John was imprisoned in the fortress of Machaerus for about eighteen months. Machaerus was a very formidable place, situated on a hill overlooking the Dead Sea. It had been built by Herod the Great, and it was virtually impregnable. There were unscaleable cliffs on three sides, and around the summit of the hill Herod had built a wall with towers at each corner. The fortress of Machaerus also served as a palace, and the dungeons that were hewn out of the rock were situated directly underneath the great hall, where Herod received his courtiers and held his banquets. In spite of his incarceration, John was able to receive visitors, for his disciples appeared to be able to come and go. We can only hope that, because of Herod's respect for John, conditions were not too grim for him.

"Art thou he that should come?"

It was from his isolated prison cell that John sent two of his disciples to Jesus:

"Now when John had heard in the prison the works of Christ, he sent two of his disciples, and said unto him, Art thou he that should come, or do we look for another?" (Matthew 11:2,3)

To ask Jesus whether he was "he that should come"* was to ask him whether he was the promised Messiah. Jesus himself used the same Greek phrase in Matthew

The dramatic hilltop fortress of Machaerus where John the Baptist was imprisoned

---

* "He that should come". Greek, *ho erchomenai*.

23, when speaking of the future time when at last the inhabitants of Jerusalem will accept the Lord Jesus Christ as their Messiah: "For I say unto you, Ye shall not see me henceforth, till ye shall say, Blessed is he that cometh in the name of the Lord" (Matthew 23:39).

To speak of the Messiah as the coming one is to call to mind a number of Old Testament scriptures. The very words of Jesus in Matthew 23 are a quotation from Psalm 118:26: "Blessed be he that cometh in the name of the LORD: we have blessed you out of the house of the LORD." Genesis 49 also speaks of the sceptre not departing from Judah, "Till he come whose it is (RV margin); and unto him shall the gathering of the people be" (Genesis 49:10). Ezekiel similarly spoke of the diadem and the crown being taken away from Zedekiah, that profane, wicked prince of Israel, "Until he come whose right it is; and I will give it him" (Ezekiel 21:27). John the Baptist himself had during his ministry taken up this Old Testament phraseology when speaking of the Lord Jesus Christ:

"John answered, saying unto them all, I indeed baptize you with water; but one mightier than I cometh, the latchet of whose shoes I am not worthy to unloose: he shall baptize you with the Holy Spirit and with fire." (Luke 3:16)

"This is he of whom I said, After me cometh* a man which is preferred before me: for he was before me". (John 1:30)

This being so, it is difficult to imagine that John, the greatest of the prophets, was really in any doubt as to the Messiahship of Jesus. He had after all received direct confirmation from heaven that Jesus was the Messiah who would baptize with Holy Spirit. John himself said, "he that sent me to baptize with water, the same said unto me, Upon whom thou shalt see the Spirit descending, and remaining on him, the same is he which baptizeth with the Holy Spirit. And I saw, and bare

* "Cometh". Greek, *erchomai*.

record that this is the Son of God" (John 1:33,34). Why, then, did John ask this question of Jesus? Could it have been for the disciples' benefit, whom John sent to enquire of Jesus? Perhaps the incarceration of John had led to doubts in the minds of his disciples. It is not difficult to imagine how these doubts might have arisen. For example, John had declared Jesus to be "the Lamb of God, which taketh away the sin of the world", but as yet there seemed to be little evidence of Jesus fulfilling this role. Furthermore, where was the baptism of Holy Spirit and fire that John had spoken of? Perhaps most pointed of all, if Jesus really was the one that should come, why was John, their master, left to languish in prison? Such misgivings as these may well have been encouraged by the Jewish authorities, who had already been guilty of seeking to drive a wedge between the disciples of John and the Lord Jesus Christ, over the matter of purifying (John 3:25,26).

Jesus' reply

At first, Jesus did not respond to their question, but carried on with his work of healing: "And in that same hour he cured many of their infirmities and plagues, and of evil spirits; and unto many that were blind he gave sight" (Luke 7:21). By the time Jesus addressed their question directly, the mighty works that the disciples of John had witnessed would surely have convinced them that Jesus was indeed the Messiah.

Notice the gentleness of Jesus' reply: there was no stinging criticism for lack of faith. Instead, he directed John's disciples to a number of prophetic scriptures from Isaiah, which were calculated to give them confirmation of his Messiahship, whilst at the same time giving to John a personal message of hope and encouragement:

"Jesus answered and said unto them, Go and shew John again those things which ye do hear and see: the blind receive their sight, and the lame walk, the lepers are cleansed, and the deaf hear, the dead are raised up, and the poor have the gospel preached to them.

87

And blessed is he, whosoever shall not be offended in me." (Matthew 11:4-6)

There are at least four allusions here to the prophecy of Isaiah, each one of them very relevant to the circumstances of John.

1. Isaiah 35

"Then the eyes of the blind shall be opened, and the ears of the deaf shall be unstopped. Then shall the lame man leap as an hart, and the tongue of the dumb sing: for in the wilderness shall waters break out, and streams in the desert." (Isaiah 35:5,6)

How relevant this was to the ministry of John, whose mission was to "prepare in the wilderness the way of the Lord". Here was consolation for John and his disciples that the purpose of his ministry would be fulfilled; the barren desolate wilderness that was Israel would one day blossom as the rose.

Notice the encouragement that is given:

"Strengthen ye the weak hands, and confirm the feeble knees. Say to them that are of a fearful heart, Be strong, fear not: behold, your God will come with vengeance, even God with a recompence; he will come and save you." (Isaiah 35:3,4)

This will be true ultimately for John. He may not have escaped the sword of the executioner, but his salvation is assured.

2. Isaiah 42

"I the LORD have called thee in righteousness, and will hold thine hand, and will keep thee, and give thee for a covenant of the people, for a light of the Gentiles; to open the blind eyes, to bring out the prisoners from the prison, and them that sit in darkness out of the prison house." (Isaiah 42:6,7)

Here is confirmation that Jesus would be given "for a covenant of the people". John declared him to be the Lamb of God to take away the sin of the world – and so he would in good time.

Whilst Isaiah 42:7 is speaking of the response of the Gentiles to the Gospel, surely John would have taken comfort from the mention of the release of prisoners from the prison house.

3. Isaiah 61

"The Spirit of the LORD God is upon me; because the LORD hath anointed me to preach good tidings unto the meek; he hath sent me to bind up the brokenhearted, to proclaim liberty to the captives, and the opening of the prison to them that are bound."

(Isaiah 61:1)

Again, notice the reference to "liberty to the captives". Surely, this would be music to John's ears! This very scripture was quoted by Jesus in the synagogue at Capernaum, with reference to his own ministry (Luke 4:16-21).

4. Isaiah 8

"And he shall be for a sanctuary; but for a stone of stumbling and for a rock of offence to both the houses of Israel, for a gin and for a snare to the inhabitants of Jerusalem. And many among them shall stumble, and fall, and be broken, and be snared, and be taken."

(Isaiah 8:14,15)

Jesus said to John via his disciples, "Blessed is he, whosoever shall not be offended* in me". Literally this means 'to cause to stumble'. There would be many in Israel who would stumble at the stumbling-stone, and on a number of occasions the Gospel writers tell us that the Jews "were offended in him" (Matthew 13:57; 15:12; Mark 6:3). They could not accept the teaching of Jesus, and so they would be subject to the baptism of fire of which John had spoken. John's prophecies of fiery judgement would be fulfilled in due time.

---

* "Offended". Greek, *skandalizo*. Thayer, *Greek-English Lexicon of the New Testament*: "To put a stumbling-block or impediment in the way, upon which another may trip and fall; to be a stumbling-block. To cause or make to stumble".

Jesus would be "for a gin and for a snare to the inhabitants of Jerusalem". It is no coincidence that in his Mount Olivet prophecy, speaking of the impending fiery judgements of AD 70, Jesus said that "as a snare shall it come on all them that dwell on the face of the whole earth" (Luke 21:35).

"What went ye out for to see?"

As the disciples of John departed to tell John what they had seen and heard, no doubt fully convinced that Jesus was the Messiah, "he that should come", Jesus turned to the multitude and delivered a withering criticism of the people's failure to respond to John's preaching:

"And as they departed, Jesus began to say unto the multitudes concerning John, What went ye out into the wilderness to see? A reed shaken with the wind? But what went ye out for to see? A man clothed in soft raiment? Behold, they that wear soft clothing are in kings' houses. But what went ye out for to see? A prophet? Yea, I say unto you, and more than a prophet."   (Matthew 11:7-9)

The reed by the river's edge spoke of weakness. The slightest gust of wind would bruise its stem and cause it to fall over. A reed shaken by the wind was a fitting representation of a man with no strength in himself to stand firm in the face of opposition. Was this true of John? Was he the sort of man who was tossed to and fro by the wind of public opinion? Clearly not, for he had not been afraid to speak his mind on numerous occasions. The Pharisees and Sadducees were a generation of vipers and John was not afraid to say so. He was quite prepared to stand up to Herod himself in the name of the truth – even at the risk of his own life.

Unlike Herod and his courtiers who inhabited the great hall above his dungeon, John was not a man clothed in soft raiment. The contrast could not have been more striking, for he "had his raiment of camel's hair, and a leathern girdle about his loins" (Matthew 3:4). John had turned his back on materialism.

John was not just a prophet. Before he was born, the angel Gabriel foretold that he would be "great in the sight of the Lord" (Luke 1:15), and so he turned out to be. Jesus confirmed in Matthew 11:11 that he was the greatest prophet that had been born of women: "Verily I say unto you, Among them that are born of women there hath not risen a greater than John the Baptist". What a wonderful accolade to receive from the lips of the Master himself!

The assessment that the Jewish leaders had made was, however, altogether different: "And all the people that heard him, and the publicans, justified God, being baptized with the baptism of John. But the Pharisees and lawyers rejected the counsel of God against themselves, being not baptized of him" (Luke 7:29,30).

"The kingdom of heaven suffereth violence"

Jesus continues to make the point that the ministry of John heralded a great transition in the purpose of God, in keeping with his greatness as a prophet:

"And from the days of John the Baptist until now the kingdom of heaven suffereth violence, and the violent take it by force. For all the prophets and the law prophesied until John."   (Matthew 11:12,13)

The era of the law and the prophets had come to an end, and since that time the kingdom of heaven had been preached by John, and then by Jesus himself. This is the sense of the corresponding verse in Luke's Gospel:

"The law and the prophets were until John: from that time the gospel of the kingdom of God is preached, and every man entereth violently into it."
(Luke 16:16, RV)

This was the essence of John's teaching: "Repent ye: for the kingdom of heaven is at hand" (Matthew 3:2). The theme was continued, after John had been put in prison, by the Master himself:

"Now after that John was put in prison, Jesus came into Galilee, preaching the gospel of the kingdom of God, and saying, The time is fulfilled, and the kingdom of God is at hand: repent ye, and believe the gospel." (Mark 1:14,15)

How had the Gospel of the kingdom been received? Jesus said, "The kingdom of heaven suffereth violence,* and the violent take it by force".** The fiery preaching of John had been received by some in Israel with zeal, but not for the right motives. Their enthusiasm for the kingdom of God was motivated by purely political objectives – it was seen as an opportunity to break free from the tyranny of Rome, and to gain political independence from Caesar. Hopes had been raised by John's declaration that "the kingdom of heaven is at hand", and there was a belief that the kingdom of God should immediately appear. This was certainly a view held by some of the Jews a while later, when Jesus approached the city of Jerusalem:

"And as they heard these things, he added and spake a parable, because he was nigh to Jerusalem, and because they thought that the kingdom of God should immediately appear." (Luke 19:11)

Hence there was an attempt by the Jews to "come and take him by force, to make him a king". Their enthusiasm to bring in the kingdom of God by force led to acts of violence, and an attempt to take Jesus by force, and thrust the kingship upon him. But they did not appreciate that the time was not yet, and that the kingdom would not come through violence. Jesus therefore thwarted their attempts to seize him by force, and "he departed again into a mountain himself alone" (John 6:15).

---

* "Violence". Greek, *Biazo*. Thayer, *Greek-English Lexicon of the New Testament*: "To use force, to apply force: to force, inflict violence on one". Used only in Matthew 11:12 and Luke 16:16.

** "Take it by force". Greek, *Harpazo*. S. Zodhiates, *The Complete Word Study Dictionary – New Testament*: "To seize upon, spoil, snatch away ... It denotes an open act of violence in contrast to cunning and secret stealing". See also Matthew 13:19; John 6:15; 10:12,28,29; Acts 23:10.

"This is Elias, which was for to come"

Jesus had said, "For all the prophets and the law prophesied until John" (Matthew 11:13). The last of the Old Testament prophets had predicted the advent of Elijah the prophet, "before the coming of the great and dreadful day of the LORD". The purpose of his coming would be to "turn the heart of the fathers to the children, and the heart of the children to their fathers, lest I come and smite the earth with a curse" (Malachi 4:5,6). It was clearly with this prophecy in mind that the Lord continued to say concerning John, "And if ye will receive it, this is Elias, which was for to come" (Matthew 11:14).

What are we to make of Jesus' words? Was he saying that the prophet Malachi's prediction concerning the future work of Elijah had its complete fulfilment in John? Or was he saying that the ministry of John was a foreshadowing of Elijah's ministry, which is yet to come? It clearly must be the latter, because when on a later occasion Jesus was questioned by the disciples concerning the belief of the scribes that Elias must first come, he replied, "Elias truly shall first come, and restore all things" (Matthew 17:10,11). Elijah's mission is thus to restore all things, and reference to Malachi 4:4 would seem to indicate that this relates to the reinstating of the Law of Moses as a national code for Israel in the age to come: "Remember ye the law of Moses my servant, which I commanded unto him in Horeb for all Israel, with the statutes and judgments." John the Baptist did not "restore all things"; in fact his ministry emphasized the inadequacy of the Law of Moses as a means of personal salvation. Furthermore this later discussion between Jesus and the disciples took place after John had been put to death. We should also bear in mind that when the Jews categorically asked John whether he was Elias, he replied, "I am not" (John 1:21). It is true that John came "in the spirit and power of Elias" (Luke 1:17), in fulfilment of the words of the angel Gabriel, and this was the point that Jesus was making when he said of John, "This is Elias, which was for to

93

come". Nevertheless there remains a future work for Elijah the prophet to accomplish, before the coming of the great and dreadful day of the Lord*.

"Children sitting in the markets"

"If ye will receive it, this is Elias, which was for to come". For the most part, they were not willing to receive it, for the greatest prophet born among women, who had come in the spirit and power of Elijah, had been taken with the connivance of the Jewish authorities and cast into prison. This is the implication behind the later words of Jesus concerning John: "But I say unto you, that Elias is come already, and they knew him not, but have done unto him whatsoever they listed. Likewise shall also the Son of man suffer of them" (Matthew 17:12). Jesus therefore delivers a parable in which he expresses his judgement of that perverse generation for the way they had responded to John, and were also responding to him.

"But whereunto shall I liken this generation?" He draws a suitable comparison with a playground game that children of his day used to play:

"It is like unto children sitting in the markets, and calling unto their fellows, and saying, We have piped unto you, and ye have not danced; we have mourned unto you, and ye have not lamented. For John came neither eating nor drinking, and they say, He hath a devil. The Son of man came eating and drinking, and they say, Behold a man gluttonous, and a winebibber, a friend of publicans and sinners. But wisdom is justified of her children." (Matthew 11:16-19)

The general meaning of Jesus' parable is clear. Whilst their message was the same, the style of the preaching of John and Jesus was very different. John lived a very austere lifestyle, and his message was uncompromising and unpalatable to many. He preached with a burning zeal, and had no time for those who did not bring forth

---

* For an exposition of Elijah's future work, see J. Thomas, "The Mystery of the Covenant of the Holy Land Explained", *Herald of the Kingdom and Age to Come*, 1855, vol. 5, pages 241-247.

fruits meet for repentance. The official verdict of the Jews concerning John was that he was mad: "He hath a devil". Jesus, on the other hand, was happy to keep company with men and women from all different walks of life. He would accept hospitality from Pharisees, as well as befriending the loathed publicans and outcasts of society. Whilst there was no compromise in his teaching, he was willing to preach the Gospel to all, both rich and poor, humble and proud. This approach also brought condemnation from the Jews: "Behold a man gluttonous, and a winebibber, a friend of publicans and sinners". Thus they rejected the two greatest preachers the world has ever seen, to their own condemnation. The baptism of fire of which John spoke would assuredly fall upon that evil generation.

9

"BEHOLD, I SEND MY MESSENGER"

FROM his prison cell, John sent his disciples to Jesus to determine whether or not he was the Messiah: "Art thou he that should come, or do we look for another?" (Matthew 11:3). By the mighty works that he performed, Jesus was able to demonstrate powerfully to the disciples of John that he was indeed the Messiah. This was reinforced by the words that Jesus spoke to John's disciples, and the numerous allusions to the prophecy of Isaiah that Jesus' words contained.

But what conclusions would the multitudes draw from the question that the disciples of John had asked? Would they conclude that John no longer believed Jesus to be the Messiah? Would doubt be cast upon John's claim to be a prophet sent from God? It was probably for this reason that Jesus chose this particular time to speak to the multitudes about John, and to affirm that John was indeed the greatest of the prophets: "Verily I say unto you, Among them that are born of women there hath not risen a greater than John the Baptist." Jesus confirmed this assessment of John by reference to Malachi 3: "For this is he, of whom it is written, Behold, I send my messenger before thy face, which shall prepare thy way before thee" (Matthew 11:10,11). This is a key Old Testament prophecy concerning the work of John the Baptist, and it is deserving of careful consideration.

Where is the God of judgement?

An appreciation of the historical background to the prophecy of Malachi will help us to understand the meaning of that section of the prophecy that relates to the work of John the Baptist. We can conclude with reasonable certainty that the prophecy was given around the time of the second return of Nehemiah to Jerusalem, recorded in Nehemiah 13. It is evident that Malachi prophesied after the rebuilding of the temple, because mention is made of the temple in Malachi 1:10 and 3:10. There are also three notable similarities between the days of Malachi and the time of Nehemiah's second return:

1) The tithes had been neglected (Nehemiah 13:10; Malachi 3:8).

2) The people of Israel had taken wives of the heathen nations (Nehemiah 13:23; Malachi 2:11-17).

3) The priesthood had been defiled (Nehemiah 13:29; Malachi 1:7-12; 2:8,9).

Malachi was therefore contemporary with Nehemiah, and he prophesied at a time when enthusiasm for the Truth was at a very low ebb. In his prophecy he highlighted the wickedness of the nation of Israel and urged them to reform. In particular, Malachi had a special rebuke for the priesthood, whose duty it was to "keep knowledge", and to teach the nation of Israel God's laws, as "the messenger of the LORD of hosts" (Malachi 2:7). They had singularly failed to discharge this responsibility, as is clear from Malachi's rebuke: "Ye are departed out of the way; ye have caused many to stumble at the law; ye have corrupted the covenant of Levi, saith the LORD of hosts" (verse 8). As a consequence of this failure by the priests, there was apostasy in Israel generally, to such a degree that there were some in Israel who had concluded that God no longer cared whether men were good or evil – that in effect He was impotent to bring judgement upon the ungodly:

"Ye have wearied the LORD with your words. Yet ye say, Wherein have we wearied him? When ye say, Every one that doeth evil is good in the sight of the LORD, and he delighteth in them; or, Where is the God of judgment?" (verse 17)

This was a very similar perspective to that adopted by the apostate members of the first century ecclesia, to whom Peter wrote his second epistle. Casting doubts upon God's intention to judge the ungodly, they said, "Where is the promise of his coming? For since the fathers fell asleep, all things continue as they were from the beginning of the creation" (2 Peter 3:4).

My messenger

God's answer to such people as this was in Malachi chapter 3. God was a God of judgement, and judgement would fall upon the ungodly. He says:

> "And I will come near to you to judgment; and I will be a swift witness against the sorcerers, and against the adulterers, and against false swearers, and against those that oppress the hireling in his wages, the widow, and the fatherless, and that turn aside the stranger from his right, and fear not me, saith the LORD of hosts." (verse 5)

Whilst God is longsuffering, He is also a God of judgement and will not clear the guilty.

Against this background of coming judgement, God now says to Israel: "Behold, I will send my messenger, and he shall prepare the way before me" (verse 1). This verse is quoted in Matthew, Mark and Luke with reference to John the Baptist. John too in his Gospel alludes to it when he says that "there was a man sent from God, whose name was John" (1:6). When John the Baptist, God's messenger, finally came, much of what he preached had to do with judgement to come, in keeping with the overall theme of Malachi's prophecy:

> "And now also the axe is laid unto the root of the trees: therefore every tree which bringeth not forth good fruit is hewn down, and cast into the fire ... he that cometh after me ... shall baptize you with the Holy Spirit, and with fire: whose fan is in his hand, and he will throughly purge his floor, and gather his wheat into the garner; but he will burn up the chaff with unquenchable fire." (Matthew 3:10-12)

A sudden coming to his temple

It is in this context of the ministry of John that God then says:

> "And the Lord, whom ye seek, shall suddenly come to his temple, even the messenger of the covenant, whom ye delight in: behold, he shall come, saith the LORD of hosts." (verse 1)

The "messenger of the covenant" is a reference to the Lord Jesus Christ, for whom John the Baptist was to prepare the way. A play on words is being used, for Malachi's name means, "My messenger".

Malachi here is using the language of irony. The people to whom he was speaking did not really seek the Lord, or delight in Him at all. On the contrary, they didn't believe in Him. But whether they believed or not, the Lord would come – and come suddenly.

When would the Lord Jesus Christ, the messenger of the covenant, come to his temple suddenly? Bearing in mind that the context of the prophecy is that of coming judgement, the answer is AD 70 when Jesus came in judgement against that wayward nation because of their rejection of him when he walked in their midst. The temple, in which the Jews placed so much trust, was destroyed in fulfilment of Jesus' words in his Mount Olivet prophecy:

> "And Jesus said unto them, See ye not all these things? Verily I say unto you, There shall not be left here one stone upon another, that shall not be thrown down." (Matthew 24:2)

This is also clearly what Stephen was preaching about in Acts 6, to his ultimate cost:

> "And they stirred up the people, and the elders, and the scribes, and came upon him, and caught him, and brought him to the council, and set up false witnesses, which said, This man ceaseth not to speak blasphemous words against this holy place, and the law: for we have heard him say, that this Jesus of

A model of Herod's temple

Nazareth shall destroy this place, and shall change the customs which Moses delivered us." (verses 12-14)

The "holy place" with which the Jews were so concerned was a reference to the temple in Jerusalem. Stephen was saying that the Lord Jesus would come and destroy that place, and do away with the Mosaic institution once and for all, because he was the "messenger of the covenant", that is, the New Covenant in his blood.

Mark's record of the Olivet prophecy is also relevant to what Malachi says about the Lord's sudden coming to his temple. Jesus appears to quote this when, by means of a parable, he exhorted his disciples to watch for the coming of that dreadful day of judgement:

"For the Son of man is as a man taking a far journey, who left his house, and gave authority to his servants, and to every man his work, and commanded the porter to watch. Watch ye therefore: for ye know not when the master of the house cometh, at even, or at midnight, or at the cockcrowing, or in the morning:

lest coming suddenly he find you sleeping. And what I say unto you I say unto all, Watch." (Mark 13:34-37)

There are of course valuable lessons for us to take from what Jesus says here as we wait for his second advent. Just as the disciples had to be ever watchful for the day of impending judgement, so must we. Nevertheless we must always be faithful to the context of scripture, and not seek to impose upon the words of Jesus a meaning that they do not have.

"Who may abide the day of his coming?"

Malachi then says:

"But who may abide the day of his coming? And who shall stand when he appeareth? For he is like a refiner's fire, and like fullers' soap." (Malachi 3:2)

The coming of the Son of man in judgement against the nation would be a time of great distress, and few would abide that terrible day. The Lord Jesus alludes to Malachi 3:2 in his Mount Olivet prophecy, when he exhorts the faithful to watch for the signs of coming judgement: "Watch ye therefore, and pray always, that ye may be accounted worthy to escape all these things that shall come to pass, and *to stand before the Son of man*" (Luke 21:36). To escape the judgements that were to be meted out upon the nation was to "stand before the Son of man".

Purify the sons of Levi

The theme of judgement is continued in Malachi chapter 3:

"For he is like a refiner's fire, and like fullers' soap: and he shall sit as a refiner and purifier of silver: and he shall purify the sons of Levi, and purge them as gold and silver, that they may offer unto the LORD an offering in righteousness." (verses 2,3)

Purification can be achieved in one of two ways – either by the cleansing of fire, or the washing of water. Malachi uses the symbolism of both here. It is significant that the baptism of John brought the cleansing of remission of

101

sins through immersion in water, and also that the theme of cleansing by fire formed a major part of the preaching of John the Baptist. The threshing-floor of Jerusalem was to be purged by the baptism of fire, whereby the chaff would be burned up:

"I indeed baptize you with water unto repentance: but he that cometh after me is mightier than I, whose shoes I am not worthy to bear: he shall baptize you with the Holy Spirit, and with fire: whose fan is in his hand, and he will throughly purge his floor, and gather his wheat into the garner; but he will burn up the chaff with unquenchable fire." (Matthew 3:11,12)

Whilst Malachi's prophecy spoke about Israel's judgements at the hand of the Romans in AD 70, this was neither the end nor indeed the beginning of the process of Israel's purification as God's people. From the very beginning of Israel's growth into a nation they were tried in "the iron furnace of Egypt" (Deuteronomy 4:20; Jeremiah 11:4). Isaiah compared the afflictions that Israel suffered in his days to the process whereby precious metal is refined:

"Behold, I have refined thee, but not with silver; I have chosen thee in the furnace of affliction. For mine own sake, even for mine own sake, will I do it: for how should my name be polluted? And I will not give my glory unto another." (Isaiah 48:10,11)

Ezekiel too compared Israel's iniquity to dross that had to be removed by the process of refinement in fire:

"And the word of the LORD came unto me, saying, Son of man, the house of Israel is to me become dross: all they are brass, and tin, and iron, and lead, in the midst of the furnace; they are even the dross of silver. Therefore thus saith the LORD God; because ye are all become dross, behold, therefore I will gather you into the midst of Jerusalem. As they gather silver, and brass, and iron, and lead, and tin, into the midst of the furnace, to blow the fire upon it, to melt it; so will I gather you in mine anger and in my fury, and I will leave you there, and melt you. Yea, I will gather you,

102

and blow upon you in the fire of my wrath, and ye shall be melted in the midst thereof. As silver is melted in the midst of the furnace, so shall ye be melted in the midst thereof; and ye shall know that I the LORD have poured out my fury upon you."   (Ezekiel 22:17-22)

Ezekiel's prophecy had specific reference to the judgements that were carried out by Nebuchadnezzar king of Babylon. To this day, the Jewish people remain a faithless, stiffnecked people, and so more purification will be required in the future. The prophet Jeremiah indicates that Israel's future affliction will be unsurpassed, yet will ultimately end in deliverance:

"Ask ye now, and see whether a man doth travail with child? wherefore do I see every man with his hands on his loins, as a woman in travail, and all faces are turned into paleness? Alas! for that day is great, so that none is like it: it is even the time of Jacob's trouble; but he shall be saved out of it."   (Jeremiah 30:6,7)

Thus there is a purpose to all of Israel's afflictions. There is an end in view, and Malachi tells us what that is:

"And he shall sit as a refiner and purifier of silver: and he shall purify the sons of Levi, and purge them as gold and silver, that they may offer unto the LORD an offering in righteousness."   (Malachi 3:3)

"I will be with thee"

Malachi's prophecy now moves forward to a consideration of the kingdom of God. It is in the kingdom age that Israel will ultimately offer acceptable worship to their God: "Then shall the offering of Judah and Jerusalem be pleasant unto the LORD, as in the days of old, and as in former years" (Malachi 3:4). No longer will they offer the lame, the torn and the sick, and say "the table of the LORD is polluted", but they will offer acceptable offerings unto God. Ezekiel too speaks of this future time when Israel's worship will be a sweet savour to God:

"For in mine holy mountain, in the mountain of the height of Israel, saith the Lord GOD, there shall all the house of Israel, all of them in the land, serve me: there will I accept them, and there will I require your offerings, and the firstfruits of your oblations, with all your holy things. I will accept you with your sweet savour, when I bring you out from the people, and gather you out of the countries wherein ye have been scattered; and I will be sanctified in you before the heathen." (Ezekiel 20:40,41)

Although the people of Israel have again to be tried in the furnace of affliction, God gives them the assurance that ultimately they shall be saved out of it. He is with them in all their afflictions:

"But now thus saith the LORD that created thee, O Jacob, and he that formed thee, O Israel, Fear not: for I have redeemed thee, I have called thee by thy name; thou art mine. When thou passest through the waters, I will be with thee; and through the rivers, they shall not overflow thee: when thou walkest through the fire, thou shalt not be burned; neither shall the flame kindle upon thee. For I am the LORD thy God, the Holy One of Israel, thy Saviour." (Isaiah 43:1-3)

This we know to be true. God will not make a full end of His people. Nevertheless He will correct them in measure, and not leave them altogether unpunished (Jeremiah 46:28; 30:11).

Purification by washing

Isaiah indicates, in the passage quoted above, that Israel would have to pass through the fire and through the waters. Two different figures of speech are being used to describe their cleansing. Likewise, Malachi says: "For he is like a refiner's fire, and like fullers' soap" (Malachi 3:2). These same two aspects of Israel's refining can be found in Isaiah 4:

"In that day shall the branch* of the LORD be beautiful and glorious, and the fruit of the earth shall be excellent and comely for them that are escaped of

---

* Hebrew, *tsamach*. See previous comments on page 25 and footnote.

Israel. And it shall come to pass, that he that is left in Zion, and he that remaineth in Jerusalem, shall be called holy, even every one that is written among the living in Jerusalem: when the LORD shall have *washed away the filth* of the daughters of Zion, and shall have purged the blood of Jerusalem from the midst thereof by the spirit of judgment, and *by the spirit of burning*."

(Isaiah 4:2-4)

This is the day for which we hope and pray, when Jerusalem shall be "holiness unto the LORD", and when "the branch of the LORD" will be beautiful and glorious.

10

THE DEATH OF JOHN

MATTHEW records the death of John at the hands of Herod in chapter 14. It was Herod's birthday, so following the example laid down in Old Testament times by Pharaoh (Genesis 40:20), he chose to celebrate the occasion with revelry and excess. He "made a supper to his lords, high captains, and chief estates of Galilee" (Mark 6:21). The sordid events that were to unfold that day would be witnessed by all the great men of state in Herod's dominion, and it is significant that the scripture gives no indication of anyone present raising a voice in protest at the actions of Herod.

Salome dances before Herod

Some time during the proceedings, no doubt when Herod's state of mind had been clouded by the soporific effects of alcohol, "the daughter of Herodias danced before them, and pleased Herod" (Matthew 14:6). The scriptures do not give her name, but secular history tells us that she was a girl called Salome, the daughter of Herodias by her first marriage to Herod Philip. She is thought

Salome

to have been about seventeen at this point when she danced before Herod, who rashly promised her with an oath anything she desired: "And he sware unto her, Whatsoever thou shalt ask of me, I will give it thee, unto the half of my kingdom" (Mark 6:23). Perhaps with an inflated opinion of his own importance, there seems to have been a deliberate intention to draw a comparison with the actions of Ahasuerus the king of Persia, when

Esther drew near to him to plead for the life of her fellow men:

"Then said the king unto her, What wilt thou, queen Esther? And what is thy request? It shall be even given thee to the half of the kingdom."

(Esther 5:3,6; 7:2)

But the contrast between Esther and Salome could not be more striking. Maybe the whole occasion had been organized with the example of king Ahasuerus in mind, for some time earlier he too had "made a feast unto all his princes and his servants; the power of Persia and Media, the nobles and princes of the provinces, being before him" (1:3). Vashti, the wife of the king, chose not to attend, but instead she "made a feast for the women in the royal house which belonged to king Ahasuerus" (1:9). Likewise Herodias was conspicuous by her absence. Nevertheless it is clear that the whole event was under her control, and had been carefully orchestrated with one objective in mind.

Herodias and Salome

Herodias hated John with a passion, because of his public denunciation of her illicit union with Herod Antipas. She knew that her position within the household would be at risk while John was allowed to live and continue his private interviews with the king, and so she planned his demise. For a long time she had desired to murder John, but hitherto had been prevented by Herod who paradoxically had a respect for him, and "kept him safe".

Salome was in collusion with her mother. Matthew tells us that she had been "before instructed of her mother" (Matthew 14:8). As soon as Herod made his rash oath, Salome "went forth, and said unto her mother, What shall I ask?" (Mark 6:24). Perhaps still showing some of the naivety of youth, she was willing to be guided by her mother in the request that she was to make before Herod.

107

But there was no naivety in the way that she approached the king. She clearly approved of Herodias' suggestion, and could see the wisdom of her response. After all, what good would half of the kingdom be to her if John the Baptist was still alive? Her position within the household would only be secure when he had gone, for she was not the daughter of Herod. And so "she came in *straightway with haste* unto the king, and asked, saying, I will that thou give me by and by in a charger the head of John the Baptist" (Mark 6:25).

The weakness of Herod

What was Herod to do? How foolish of him to swear with an oath to this young girl in front of so many witnesses. He would have done well to have heeded the words of the Lord Jesus himself:

> "Again, ye have heard that it hath been said by them of old time, Thou shalt not forswear thyself, but shalt perform unto the Lord thine oaths: but I say unto you, Swear not at all; neither by heaven; for it is God's throne: nor by the earth; for it is his footstool: neither by Jerusalem; for it is the city of the great King. Neither shalt thou swear by thy head, because thou canst not make one hair white or black. But let your communication be, Yea, yea; Nay, nay: for whatsoever is more than these cometh of evil." (Matthew 5:33-37)

But now the damage was done. To comply with Salome's request was unthinkable, but having sworn with an oath to her, he would lose all credibility before his guests if he failed to keep his word.

The right course of action at this stage would have been to admit that he had made an error, and refuse the request. Herod was essentially a weak king. Whilst he had a regard and a respect for John, and heard him gladly, he was not able or willing to stand up to the evil machinations of his wife. The executioner was duly sent, and John's head was brought and given to Salome, who gave it to her mother.

John's burial

When news leaked out to John's disciples, they came and took the body and buried it. With great poignancy the record says that they "went and told Jesus" (Matthew 14:12). Deprived of their beloved leader, where else could they go? No doubt Jesus would have comforted their hearts, and spoken to them of the certainty of John's resurrection from the dead at the last day. Their actions are a valuable lesson for us. In our times of trouble and distress we should do well to follow their example, and cast all our cares and anxieties upon the Lord, knowing that He cares for us.

What happened to the family of Herod?

It is fitting that all three parties that had a hand in the death of John met an ignominious end. In AD 38, after the death of Tiberius, Herod Antipas travelled to Rome in an attempt to procure a royal title from the Emperor Caligula. Herod Agrippa, who was very much in favour with Caligula, opposed this, with the result that Herod Antipas was condemned to banishment at Lugdunum in Gaul. He eventually died in Spain. Herodias was offered a pardon, and the emperor offered her a present of money, advising her that Herod Agrippa had pleaded on her behalf. She refused this offer, and voluntarily chose to share the exile of her husband.

Salome ultimately married Philip, the tetrarch of Trachonitis, her paternal uncle, who died childless. She then married her cousin Aristobulus, by whom she had three sons. It is thought that she accompanied Herod Antipas and Herodias in their banishment. With awful irony, tradition has it that as they journeyed into Spain Salome passed over a river that was frozen. The ice broke under her feet and she sank in up to her neck. When the ice re-formed she remained suspended by it, and ultimately was decapitated, thus suffering the same death that she had brought upon John the Baptist.

109

Manaen

We are given the story of John's death in great detail – almost as if an eyewitness had been present. And why did the disciples of John have such free access to his body in and out of the fortress at Machaerus? Perhaps there is an explanation in Acts 13:

"Now there were in the church that was at Antioch certain prophets and teachers; as Barnabas, and Simeon that was called Niger, and Lucius of Cyrene, and Manaen, which had been brought up with Herod the tetrarch, and Saul." (Acts 13:1)

Manaen was a believer in the ecclesia at Antioch, and he he had been brought up with Herod. The Revised Version says he was Herod's "foster brother". Could it be that he was the source of information for the Gospel writers concerning John's death? Was he present when John and Herod talked together? Was he instrumental in getting John's disciples safely in and out of the fortress? What is clearly the case is that this man responded wholeheartedly to the teaching of John, unlike Herod himself, and he embraced the Truth. Ultimately he took that Truth all the way to Antioch. One day soon he will meet John again, and they will both see the Lord Jesus Christ, and John will realise at last that Jesus accomplished everything that John said he would. May that day soon come.

SCRIPTURE INDEX

111

113

JOHN THE BAPTIST

BIBLIOGRAPHY

J. Allfree   *A World Destroyed By Fire*
Bible Study Publications,
Mansfield, UK, 2006

M. Anstey   *Chronology of the Old Testament*
Kregel Publications, Grand
Rapids, Michigan, USA, 1973

W. F. Barling   *Law and Grace*
CMPA, Birmingham, UK, 1952

H. Balz &   *Exegetical Dictionary of the*
G. Schneider   *New Testament*
Eerdmans Publishing Company,
Grand Rapids, Michigan, USA,
1982

A. Barnes   *Barnes on the New Testament*,
Volume 1, *Matthew & Mark*
Blackie & Son, London, UK, 1832

J. J. Blunt   *Undesigned Scriptural*
Coincidences
CMPA, Birmingham, UK, 1983

J. Carter   *Parables of the Messiah*
CMPA, Birmingham, UK, 1947

A. Edersheim   *The Life and Times of Jesus the*
Messiah
Hendrickson Publishers, Inc., 1993

A. Edersheim   *The Temple, Its Ministry and*
Services as They Were at the Time
of Jesus Christ
The Religious Tract Society,
London, UK

W. Gesenius — *Hebrew-Chaldee Lexicon to the Old Testament*
Baker Book House, Grand Rapids, Michigan, USA, 1979

F. Godet — *Commentary on Luke's Gospel*
T & T Clark, Edinburgh, UK, 1870

F. Josephus — *Complete Works*
Pickering and Inglis Ltd, London, UK, 1960

G. Kittel — *Theological Dictionary of the New Testament*
Eerdmans Publishing Company, Grand Rapids, Michigan, USA, 1964

J. B. Lightfoot — *St. Paul's Epistles to the Colossians and to Philemon*
Zondervan Publishing House, Grand Rapids, Michigan, USA, 1961

J. Martin — *The Schoolmaster – An Exposition of the Book of Leviticus*
Christadelphian Scripture Study Service, Hawthorndene, South Australia, 2005

A. H. Nicholls — *The Evangelical Revival – A Modern Challenge to Biblical Truth*
CMPA, Birmingham, UK, 1983

R. Roberts — *Dr. Thomas, His Life and Work*
CMPA, Birmingham, UK, 1980

J. Strong — *Exhaustive Concordance*
Baker Book House, Grand Rapids, Michigan, USA, 1977

JOHN THE BAPTIST

J. H. Thayer	*Greek-English Lexicon of the New Testament* Baker Book House, Grand Rapids, Michigan, USA, 1977
J. Thomas	*Exposition of Daniel* CMPA, Birmingham, UK, 1978
J. Thomas	"The Mystery of the Covenant of the Holy Land Explained" *Herald of the Kingdom and Age to Come*, Volume 5, New York, USA, 1855
J. Thomas	"The Baptism of Fire" *The Christadelphian*, Volume 10, Birmingham, UK, 1873
J. Thomas	*The Last Days of Judah's Commonwealth* Logos Publications, West Beach, South Australia, 1981
W. E. Vine	*Expository Dictionary of New Testament Words* Oliphants Inc., USA, 1952
B. Wilson	*Emphatic Diaglott* The Abrahamic Faith Beacon Publishing Society, Miami, Florida, USA, 2004
S. Zodhiates	*The Complete Word Study Dictionary – New Testament* AMG Publishers, Chattanooga, USA, 1992